GHOST TOWNS OF ONTARIO

Volume 2

Ron Brown

Cannonbooks

Cannonbooks

25 Connell Court, Unit 2
Toronto, Ontario
M8Z 1E8

Canadian Cataloguing in Publication Data

Brown, Ron, 1945-
  Ghost towns of Ontario

Previous ed. in one volume only.
ISBN 0-9691210-2-4 (v. 1). — ISBN 0-9691210-1-6 (v. 2).

1. Cities and towns, Ruined, extinct, etc.—Ontario.
2. Ontario—History. I. Title.

FC3061.B76 1983   971.3'03   C83-098571-9
F1057.B76 1983

Printed in Canada by
imprimerie gagné ltée

7th Printing — August 1991

**Cover photo: An abandoned general store at Mine Centre,
northern Ontario.**

TABLE OF CONTENTS

AUTHOR'S NOTE.. 5
INTRODUCTION.. 7

SECTION ONE

SOUTHERN ONTARIO..... 9

ST. JOSEPH... 12
WROXETER 16
ABERDEEN 18
MALCOLM... 20
GILLIES HILL 22
GLAMMIS.. 24
PORT MILFORD.. 27
PETWORTH 29
CHEDDAR 31
GELERT.. 33

SECTION TWO

COTTAGE COUNTRY........ 35

MOWAT... 38
SEGUIN FALLS 45
DEPOT HARBOUR.. 47
COCKBURN ISLAND..................................... 51
GEORGIAN BAY FISHING ISLANDS 56
SPANISH MILLS.. 62
MOYLES MILLS 66
MICHAELS BAY 68
FRENCH RIVER.. 71
SPRAGGE 74
VICTORIA MINES.. 78
OPHIR 81
ARDBEG 84
LOST CHANNEL/PAKESLEY 87
BRENT... 91
KIOSK/FOSMILL... 94

SECTION THREE
NORTHERN ONTARIO..... 99

JACKFISH... 101
NICHOLSON... 105
DALTON MILLS AND DALTON STATION........... 111
TIONAGA... 114
TOPHET 116
SILVER CENTRE....................................... 119
SILVER ISLET... 125
SILVER MOUNTAIN.................................... 130
MINE CENTRE 133
GOLD ROCK... 141
BURCHELL LAKE...................................... 146
BANKFIELD 150
LEITCH 153
THERESA.. 155
PICKLE CROW/CENTRAL PATRICIA 157
UCHI LAKE.. 161
BERENS RIVER 164

EPILOGUE... 168
GLOSSARY... 169
PHOTO CREDITS 170
BIBLIOGRAPHY 171
INDEX... 173

AUTHOR'S NOTE

This book is both a companion to and a replacement for the first volume, *Ghost Towns of Ontario, Volume One*. While that volume recounted the rollicking adventures of southern Ontario's vanished villages and relic hamlets, *Volume Two* embarks upon a different adventure. It visits all Ontario—the remote and romantic mining towns of the north, the abandoned sawmill towns of cottage country and the photogenic partial ghost towns of southern Ontario. These empty and part-empty towns all contain ghostly remnants of their heyday.

While *Volume One* was for the armchair historian and the recreational driver, this volume is for the adventurer and the photographer. Some sites are remote, their access a challenge; others are drive-in. But for the intrepid "ghost-towner", the rewards at the end are the shells of the headframes or wharves of another day.

More hands than mine helped prepare this book. So little has been published on the fascinating history of Ontario's north, although this is rapidly changing, that for much of my information I went straight to its inhabitants. Their response was immediate and generous. District staff of the Ministry of Natural Resources, staff of Ontario's Ministry of Citizenship and Culture, librarians and museum curators in places like Cobalt, Terrace Bay, Bayfield, Thunder Bay, Parry Sound, Fort Frances and Dryden, municipal clerks, pulp company employees and unsuspecting residents upon whom I descended unannounced, all share credit.

Those who went that extra step deserve mention by name: Darryl Allan, curator of the Fort Frances museum; Archie Hoshino of the Ministry of Natural Resources in Geraldton; Harry Bell of Mine Centre; Rob Anderson of the Ministry of Natural Resources in Fort Frances; Viola Lewis for her history of Ardbeg; Mrs. E. Knauff, librarian in Terrace Bay; my friend Gord Wagar for his companionship on many a ghost town venture and my wife for her patience with my long absences. Thanks too to Ian Rhind and Joe McAllister for their thoughtful comments on my manuscript. All in all it was a team effort.

Ron Brown,
Toronto,
March, 1983.

INTRODUCTION

An old church leans in the waving grass. Its boards are weathered, its roof sags and its steeple tilts. A dozen cabins surround it. The only noise comes from the cawing crows that circle overhead and the shrill distant whistle of an approaching train. It may appear to be some fabled western ghost town but it is not, it is the scene at Nicholson in northeastern Ontario.

Most North American ghost towns are located where the popular imagination has placed them—in some western desert. Often they fill the preconceived image of tumble-down, false-fronted stores full of tales of shoot-outs and lost gold. Yet some appear in unexpected locales. Dozens dot the grasslands of southern Saskatchewan and the distant coves of foggy Newfoundland. They nestle in the mountain passes of British Columbia and the Yukon. And they are found everywhere in Ontario.

Most were one-industry towns. Gold, timber, even fish brought them to life. Once the shafts no longer glittered, the forests were razed or the fish no longer thrashed in the nets, the towns died.

In Saskatchewan, many were grain elevator towns that depended on the maze of railway branch lines for their survival. When the lines closed they died. Around the coast of Newfoundland, fishing operations have been centralized and many tiny outports abandoned. Mining rushes created the vacant villages of B.C. and the best known of Canada's ghost towns, Dawson City in the Yukon.

Some ghost towns are enjoying new life, not from the old industries but a new one—tourism. Bottle collectors poke through the tall grasses for onion-shaped wine bottles or glass-stopper whiskey bottles. Photographers focus their Pentaxes on weathered storefronts or church steeples while painters dab acrylic on their waiting canvas. Some are so popular they have lost all their ghostliness.

In British Columbia the old mining towns of Barkerville and Fort Steele have been reconstructed and preserved in provincial parks. The boom town buildings of Dawson City are retained in their state of suspended decay. In Val Jalbert, an early lumber town in Northern Quebec with a remarkable hotel, convent and row of 50 houses, the provincial government has worked to preserve it carefully. In Newfoundland busy tour boats cut through the choppy bays to abandoned outports to show tourists a way of life which is quickly vanishing.

In the United States desert gold-rush sites like Bodie, California have become part of state parks, while Jerome in Arizona has been preserved by gift shop and gallery owners. In Arizona, Virginia City and the notorious Tombstone have had their old stores filled with craft shops and fast-food franchises.

Ontario is in many ways unique with more, and a greater variety of ghost towns than any other Canadian province. Amid the country's best farmland in Southern Ontario, the ghosts of gristmill towns and farmer's crossroad-hamlets abound. Colonization roads that lead to rocky highlands are littered with abandoned farms and empty villages. Cottage country in central Ontario was once cloaked in stands of lofty pine, its waters abounding in fish, but when careless over-exploitation utterly depleted these resources, the sawmill towns and fishing villages died. Railways opened northern Ontario and for decades were its lifeline. Mill towns and maintenance villages lined the three transcontinental (CPR, Canadian Northern and National Transcontinental) and two development (Algoma Central, Temiskaming and Northern Ontario) lines while the railways opened the north to several gold and silver rushes. Mining towns were abandoned when the deposits ran dry, while the mill towns fell victim to two villains: over-exploitation and the invasion of the multinational pulp companies.

The condition of Ontario's ghost towns is as varied as their origin. Some appear today much as the day they were abandoned, while others have vanished with little trace. Most retain some ghostly reminders: sagging shells, chimneys, looming headframes or old road patterns. Some are maintained as seasonal communities and some have new homes. Still others are only partly abandoned. Yet they are all ghosts of their one-time prosperity.

Incredibly, Ontario's ghost towns lie ignored, unlike those in Newfoundland, Quebec, British Columbia, the Yukon or the American west. Not one is preserved; not one is publicized. Although internal Ontario government reports have identified two of the best, Nicholson and Gold Rock, and urged their preservation, the government has turned its back on them, as it has on heritage preservation in general.

It is worse than that. The government agency responsible for historical buildings on Crown Land has a policy not to preserve the old towns, the old trappers' cabins, the forestry towers or ranger stations. It burns them. Little wonder that Heritage Canada once described the Ontario government's meagre efforts as being among the weakest in the western world.

That is one of my reasons for writing this book. Perhaps by reading the story of these ghost towns, by visiting and photographing them, Ontario heritage enthusiasts may succeed in preserving one or two and elevating them to their proper place among the ghost towns of North America.

SECTION ONE

SOUTHERN ONTARIO

Southern Ontario contains Ontario's oldest ghost towns, most of them products of its long history and varied geography. Shaped like a huge triangle, its southern and northwestern sides are defined by the Great Lakes, its northeastern side by the Ottawa and French Rivers. Most of it lies covered in deep glacial deposits. The southern deposits are flat fertile lake bottoms, the heart of Ontario's farm economy. Further north the deposits become hillier and stonier until finally the soils lose out to the bare pink bedrock of an ancient mountain root known as the Canadian Shield. Large rivers meander through the plains and became Ontario's early highways and power sites.

Other than scattered fur posts and French forts, southern Ontario had no permanent villages prior to the British conquest in 1759. Until the American revolution raised the spectre of enemy invasion, the British ignored these remote forests. Then a new governor, John Graves Simcoe, built a chain of small forts linked by roads and established around them farmers and artisans who could provide the necessary manpower, food and hardware to feed any future military conflict.

The American revolution brought about Ontario's first concerted settlement by the United Empire Loyalists. For supporting the English or for simply failing to support the rebels, many Americans were stripped of their land and money and fled to Canada. To reward their loyalty the British in 1783 surveyed ten townships along the shores of the St. Lawrence River and eastern Lake Ontario for the refugees. Others settled at Niagara and Detroit. Their first villages usually consisted of a sawmill, hotel, store, port facilities and a handful of frame homes.

Thirty years of colonization followed. Among the first settlers were disbanded Scottish regiments who received lands in eastern Ontario along the St. Lawrence and Rideau Rivers. The Lanark Societies and Peter Robinson brought poverty-striken emigrants from Scotland and Ireland and led them to the counties of Lanark and Peterborough. Meanwhile at the western end, Colonel Thomas Talbot, and the Canada Company under John Galt and Tiger Dunlop, were busy selling land between Lakes Erie and Huron. Some settlements were failures. William Berczy's Germans who tried to establish a colony north of what is now Toronto lasted only a few years as did the French Royalist De Puisaye and his French aristocrats who had fled sure death in post-revolutionary France. Other settlements were religious. A group of Quebeckers having been crowded out of their home parishes arrived at the shores of Lake Huron near modern-day Bayfield around 1830. Amish flocked to what became the

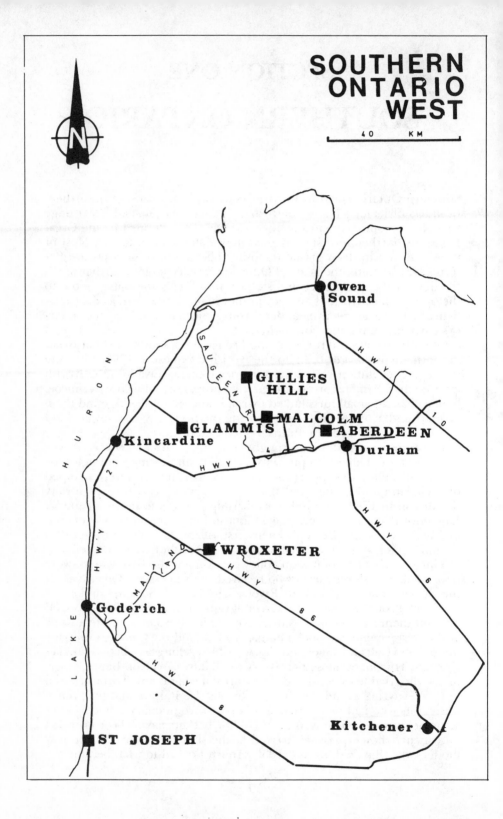

Stratford area and after 1800 the well-known Mennonites migrated from Pennsylvania to the counties of Waterloo and Markham.

Between 1830 and 1850 the backlands filled in. More than two dozen roads crept inland from the ports on Lake Ontario. Along them were a string of stopping places, usually at ten-kilometer (6-mile) or half-day intervals. Wherever the roads crossed water-power sites, sawmills were built and became the focus for village growth. Concession roads branched into the farm lots which were soon populated with pioneers. Hotels, stores, blacksmiths and churches grouped at the busier road junctions. Because the roads were dreadful, settlers could venture only short distances creating the densest network of villages and hamlets in Ontario's history.

The period from 1850 to 1880 was a time of expansion. As exports to the U. S. increased the little ports boomed. From the settled areas colonization roads shot into the bush. Roads like the Elora Road, the Garafraxa Road and the Sydenham Road pierced the Queen's Bush where the counties of Grey and Bruce now prosper, while more than a dozen such roads were laid out by the government to lure settlers into a rocky upland between the Ottawa River and Georgian Bay, known as the Ottawa-Huron Tract. The land in the Queen's Bush was fertile and the settlements prospered. In the Ottawa-Huron Tract, however, things were different. The soils between the rocky outcrops were sandy and ultimately useless and many of the settlements were quickly abandoned. It was also a time of railway building. Promoted by businessmen in the ports, the railways snaked inland and changed the face of the land once more. Villages in their path boomed into important shipping and factory towns; those that were bypassed stagnated.

At the turn of the century more villages began to vanish. The clearing of the forest cover not only exhausted the wood supply for the sawmills, but also played havoc with the flows of the smaller mill streams. Sudden spring floods washed away dams and millwheels, summer droughts ground them to a halt and many early mill villages vanished. In 1890 a harsh U. S. tariff on Canadian exports brought the end to many smaller ports. Temperance movements closed hotels, rural mail delivery replaced the general store post office, while the factory system doomed the village craftsman and the auto age the blacksmith. As a result many crossroads villages vanished from the maps.

These came to be the ghost towns of southern Ontario. Because it is an area of bustle and expansion many old buildings have been demolished to make way for the new. While most of the ghost towns in this area have some occupants in or around them, weathered buildings, vacant and boarded, still line the old streets. In them spectres of the past dominate.

ST. JOSEPH

If you search for the dream city of St. Joseph today you will inevitably end up at a small historical plaque beside the ruins of the Balmoral Hotel. There is little evidence today that here stood the foundling city of St. Joseph. The hotel was the only part of a grand scheme by would-be railway and canal builder Narcisse Cantin that was realized... and even it failed.

During the 1840s the fertile clay plains of southern Huron County stretching to the shores of Lake Huron became the destination of Quebec's crowded and poor farmers. Among them was Antoine Cantin. As the Quebeckers cut back the forests, one crude road inched down the Lake Huron shoreline and a second cut inland through the dark forests to Zurich. Near the crossroads, on a small creek, Moses Johnson built the area's first sawmill and the community became known as Johnson's Mills. The crossroads quickly attracted a church, general store, post office and tavern. In 1857 optimistic landowners laid out an impressive townsite and named their future metropolis Lakeview, but once the hamlet acquired the basic rural services its growth stopped and the townsite remained empty.

Born in 1870, Narcisse Cantin quickly established himself as an entrepreneur. By the age of 17 he was a cattle dealer shipping from the railway town of Zurich. Within a few years he was successful enough to move his operation to Buffalo. Impressed with what he saw of the Erie Canal, he began drawing up plans. He thought what Ontario needed was a series of deep canals which would bypass the rapids of the St. Lawrence and the shallow Welland canal. These canals would cross Ontario's southwest peninsula and terminate at his hometown of Lakeview. He would build a city there and bring home expatriate French Canadians who had settled in Chicago to populate it.

By 1897 his plans were finished. He had taken the old Lakeview plan and enlarged it to 400 lots and 20 streets with such exotic names as

12

The main street of St. Joseph around the turn of the century, Vallee Street, featured a large number of grand brick buildings.

Napoleon and Josephine. Park Avenue swept about a mile from the main street (the old shore road) to the lake where it ended at a huge recreational park. He called his city St. Joseph.

St. Joseph grew quickly. In less than a decade it attracted an organ factory, a winery and a brick works. There are still examples of homes built of the lovely yellow brick. Beside the old Lakeview store and hotel, there was the Bissonette Block, an office for the professional men of the town. By 1904 the city contained 25 grand homes, many of them three-storeys high and constructed of yellow brick.

The centrepiece of St. Joseph was to be the Balmoral Hotel. Cantin began construction in 1897 and poured a quarter-million dollars into it, an impressive sum worth a 100 times that now. The three-storey yellow brick hotel occupied an entire city block and boasted an 80-foot bar. Advertisements went out from a special office in New York and touted it as a grand recreational hotel.

It never opened. Although rushed to completion by 1907 (the turrets planned for the roof were not built) there were hotels in the rocky wilds of Muskoka already open and luring the tourists. Huron's flat featureless countryside could not compete with Muskoka and the hotel stood empty.

Narcisse Cantin's other dreams also remained empty. In 1906 he opened a wharf to ship lumber and fish, but waves and ice soon washed it away. He then begin to promote a new railway, the St. Joseph and Stratford Radial Railway, to link the two towns and the villages of Grand Bend and Parkhill. Unfortunately, he couldn't regain investor confidence after the debacle of the Balmoral, despite his glossy brochures. He was behind the times. The railway boom had ended.

In 1914, after 12 years of effort, he managed to incorporate the Great

The New Balmoral Hotel, as it was advertised in New York, was to be the centrepiece of St. Joseph. Although built, it never opened.

There are still examples of the pump organs which were built in this one-time organ factory. It is one of the few buildings to survive the demise of St. Joseph.

Narcisse Cantin was the man who dreamed of a city at St. Joseph which would be the terminus of a new Ontario canal and a vacation spot for the rich. His dream was never realized.

Lakes and Atlantic Canal and Power Company. Taking a leap into the future he recognized the potential of electrical power and switched his emphasis from the canal to electricity, but WWI delayed financing. During the 20s a political scandal involving the Liberal government of MacKenzie King and power development on the St. Lawrence killed the dream.

St. Joseph stagnated. One by one its businesses closed and in 1920 the Balmoral Hotel was torn down, its elegant furnishings sold to the highest bidder and the bricks used in far less grand buildings. Cantin, diminished from years of grandiose scheming followed by failure, returned to his city and watched it decline until he died in 1940.

It is still possible to find traces of Cantin's dream city. Among the prosperous towns and green fields of Huron County, at the intersection of Highways 84 and 21, about 40 kilometers (25 miles) south of Goderich lie the massive foundations of the Balmoral Hotel. Behind them lie the ruins of the Bissonette Block. Part of the organ factory is now a craft shop fronting on Park Avenue while near it lies the old Cantin home. Park Avenue still leads to the lake where a new wharf is busy with fishermen. With their poles and tackle they often pause beside the foundations of the hotel where the Ontario government has erected a plaque to the memory of Narcisse Cantin and his grand scheme.

WROXETER

On the surface there is little reason a town with 250 residents should be called a ghost town. However, the string of shut and boarded businesses which line the main street of Wroxeter provides the most striking ghosted main street in the province.

As pioneers filled the farmlands between Lakes Erie and Huron, negotiations began with Ojibway tribes for the territory between Lake Huron and Georgian Bay. Known as the Queen's Bush, it was acquired in 1836, surveyed in 1847 and finally opened to settlement in 1854.

The western portion, which became Bruce County, was generally flat with a few gently rolling hills. The Saugeen River drained the northern section into Lake Huron; the Maitland River the southern portion. Both had numerous water-power sites. At one location on the Maitland near the borders of Bruce and Huron Counties, Robert and Thomas Gibson built a saw and grist mill. From the very first, settlers needed supplies and in 1858 Andrew Patton opened a general store. Travel increased and by 1860 Wroxeter had three hotels.

Other businesses quickly followed. Blacksmiths, carriage makers, cabinet makers and tinsmiths opened in the bustling village. In 1874 the Toronto, Grey and Bruce Railway arrived. Although the station was located halfway between Wroxeter and its main rival, a town called Gorrie four kilometers (2.5 miles) east, the railway brought new industry to the town. Robert Forsyth opened a woollen mill, James Ireland a shingle mill, William Jolly a foundry, Musson and Andrews a tannery and the Clark brothers another grist mill. The most important single industry to open was Nathaniel Allen's furniture factory. For several decades it dominated the town.

The residents and businessmen of Wroxeter were eager to incorporate their village so they could collect taxes and pass bylaws. In 1875 they saw their chance. While a large number of migrant railway workers were in town, the residents called in the census takers. They counted 764 people, just over the magic number needed for village status.

Brick houses gradually replaced the first log and frame buildings. By the turn of the century the main street looked prosperous. On each side stood block upon block of brick stores. Tailors, clothing stores, shoe shops, bakeries and implement dealers hung out their signs. Buggies and wagons clattered along the dirt road while pedestrians scurried out of the way. At the end of the main street was the river. There stood the mills, tannery and furniture factory. There seemed little doubt that

16

While still largely a residential community Wroxeter today has one of Ontario's most spectacular ghosted main streets with 15 of 18 shops boarded up.

Wroxeter would rise to be one of the county's leading towns. But there were other towns whose residents were equally optimistic.

On the banks of the Maitland River a short distance from Wroxeter, a string of villages arose. Four kilometers (2.5 miles) east was Gorrie and six kilometers (3.5 miles) east, Fordwich. To the west stood Bluevale and Wingham. As the towns grew, rivalry intensified. While the surrounding farm population was at its peak in 1900 and while farmers had their travelling distances limited by poor roads and horse power, the towns could sustain their businesses despite proximity to one another. The 1920s, however, ushered in the auto age and ushered out large numbers of the farm population. The bubble burst. The customers who remained had quick access to larger towns and began to ignore Wroxeter. Gradually the hotels, mills, factories and stores shut their doors. Finally in 1948 the ultimate blow came when the town's population dropped so low it lost its status as an incorporated village.

Today the river flows beneath a new bridge, its power unharnessed by industry. On the tree-lined back streets most of the houses remain occupied, many by retirees. On the main street the desolation is complete. Of 18 businesses all but three are boarded up. Here and there old signs, broken and weathered proclaim the former tenants. Weeds poke through the cracks in the sidewalks. No cars line the curb; few people stroll in front of the one-time stores. While Wroxeter can make no claim to being a pure ghost town, the ghost town image presented by its main street is one of the most striking and photogenic this province can offer.

ABERDEEN

The Rocky Saugeen River deserves its name. As it tumbles through the rugged hills of central Grey County 110 kilometers (70 miles) northwest of Toronto its waters bubble over bouldery beds. On its banks five kilometers (3 miles) northwest of the town of Durham lie the shells, foundations and even a rusting old bridge that were once the heart of one of the Rocky Saugeen's busiest mill villages, Aberdeen.

By 1840 southern Ontario was full, its farmers clambering for more land for their sons. Emigration from Europe was increasing, especially in 1842 when the killer potato famines forced Irishmen to North America. Up until then the great wilderness northwest of Toronto, called the Queen's Bush, had remained dark, impenetrable and mysterious. It was time, the government concluded, to open it for settlement. From the town of Shelburne they pushed the Sydenham Road into the woods, from Guelph the Garafraxa Road. Both terminated at Owen Sound. As settlers trudged along them they rested at small wayside inns a half-day's travel apart — about 10 kilometers (6 miles).

Mills soon appeared wherever water power was available and the tumbling waters of the Rocky Saugeen afforded many such sites. Naturally, the first to sprout mills were those closest to the new roads.

Durham on the Garafraxa quickly grew as a mill and stopover town. Just five kilometers (3 miles) downstream M.C. Schofield constructed a sawmill in 1851. Six years later Ferguson added a grist mill which one traveller described as a "substantial stone building with 4 run of stone and abundant water power." A short distance downstream Robert Dalglish added another sawmill in 1865. Schofield's Mills, as the place was first called, became a busy focus for the area's settlers. It soon acquired all the facilities that they needed: a blacksmith, a store and a log hotel. In 1879 James Crawford bought Schofield's mill and when the post office

Aberdeen in the late 1880s was a busy sawmill town like many others, but it was one of the first to have electricity throughout the village. Hydro power was supplied by the Rocky Saugeen River.

Today's Aberdeen has little more than foundations of houses, the remains of a bridge and sawmill and this abandoned house.

arrived in 1880 Crawford, the first postmaster named it "Crawford's Mills". Three times a week wooden stagecoaches rattled over the short but rough stretch of road that linked the mill village with Durham.

Then in 1896 the village, now called Aberdeen, gained new fame. Because of the reliability of the water power it became the site of a power plant. Electricity was the invention of the day and the local population wasted little time in lighting up its homes, streets and businesses. In fact for several years the Aberdeen plant was used to light Durham and surrounding areas.

But Aberdeen's backbone remained Crawford's sawmill. It was located on the south side of the river beside the bridge, along with the large Crawford home. Across the river a string of workers' homes lined the north bank. Near the Crawford house was the intersection of two farm roads and this became the location of the store and shops.

As Aberdeen had grown with the sawmill, it also died with it. By 1935 the land had been cleared and the timber was gone. After 80 years of operation the saws fell silent. Businesses closed and the townspeople moved, most to nearby Durham. Aberdeen became a ghost town.

Although 45 years have passed since the collapse of the village, there is still much to see. The workers' road is now a lane through the woods where the foundations of their simple cabins remain. A new road alignment has bypassed the west bridge and the ancient iron structure sits rusting and unused. By the east bridge and near the one-time crossroads are the shells and overgrown lots of the shops and larger homes. The Crawford home is occupied by new tenants, but nearby the ageless Rocky Saugeen washes over the foundations of the old mill which once had harnessed it.

MALCOLM

On a quiet country crossroad amidst the flat farmlands of Grey County sits a grey, weathering house and shop. Nearby is a school house. They are all that survive of a once-busy crossroads village named Malcolm.

Until the forests had been cleared, Grey County's roads remained quagmires. Once the trees were gone and the stumps removed, the boggy land dried and the roads became passable. As more buggies and wagons rattled and creaked over the rutted roads, hamlets appeared at the busier junctions. North of Hanover at the intersection of sideroad 25 and concession road 10, Malcolm grew as one of those crossroads villages.

The businesses which were started in those villages satisfied farmers' and travellers' most immediate needs. One of the first establishments in Malcolm was McGuire's Hotel. It provided accommodation for settlers travelling to their lots and refreshment for those already there. Later a general store, blacksmith, cheese factory and community hall were built to serve local requirements. Finnerty built another hotel, while in 1873 the booming crossroads added a school and a new Presbyterian church. The post office opened in 1869 and was named after an early settler John Malcolm. At one point nearly a dozen buildings crowded the intersection.

The business directories of the day list the community's various businessmen: Lachlin McNevin was the long-time village smithy; Reverend David Duff was the Presbyterian minister; Dan Sullivan operated the

Like many other busy crossroads hamlets, Malcolm's death was foreshadowed by the first car which chugged along its muddy streets. At its height Malcolm had over a dozen buildings and was a service centre for the surrounding farm community.

20

An old school, a cemetery and these shells are all that is left of Malcolm today.

cheese factory, general store and post office. An entrepreneur, Sullivan also owned the community hall, which at various times served as a meeting hall, school house, wagon factory and paint shop.

A stage traveller in 1883 would have disembarked in front of Finnerty's tavern located on the northeast corner. He may then have ambled across the road to Sullivan's store for a plug of tobacco or stopped at the neighbouring post office for a look at the most recent newspaper. Walking south on the sideroad, beyond the store, he would have passed on his left the hall, cheese factory and a few other dwellings and on the right the church, with its cemetery, Dave Duff's manse, McNevin's blacksmith shop and simple log house.

In 1983 travellers speed through in their cars. They don't see the vacant house and shop on the northwest corner, the school on the southeast or the cemetery on the southwest—the old hamlet's sole survivors. On the grounds of Dan Sullivan's store, the Women's Institute of the area has placed a cairn which reads simply, "In memory of the pioneers of this community". The community those pioneers knew has largely vanished.

GILLIES HILL

Far to the west of Malcolm an empty church and school are all that remain of another crossroads hamlet, Gillies Hill.

Like Malcolm, Gillies Hill lay in the Queen's Bush. This woodland was the last large part of southern Ontario to be opened for settlement. Southern Bruce County contained the most fertile soils and soon was the site of a prosperous farming community.

Elderslie Township contained uniformly good soil and quickly attracted a band of Scottish settlers, many from the areas of Colonsay and Cantire. John Gillies arrived with the others in the early 1850s and in 1857 was elected the township's first reeve. He clung to office until 1873 and later served as Warden of the county and then a member of parliament in Ottawa. Although there are no hills in the area greater than gentle swales, the crossroads was called Gillies Hill.

Because of the area's remarkable fertility the community grew quickly. Between 1857 and 1875 Gillies Hill acquired a school, store, post office, blacksmith shop, township hall and a few dwellings. As the Scots Presbyterians scorned alcohol, the village never saw a hotel or tavern. For such a religious community the church was built relatively late, in 1908. Until then worship had been carried out in the township hall. Early

Gillies Hill never had much, but what it once had makes picturesque ruins today. The building in the background is not a church but the old school.

business directories showed the hamlet was a busy spot: W.A. Stevens and D. Graham operated stores, McCalder the blacksmith shop.

Following the first war many hamlets declined. The auto age allowed farmers to travel to the larger towns to shop. This along with the replacement of many rural post offices with mail delivery, sounded the death knell. Gillies Hill was no exception.

The church closed in 1936, the school in 1952 and the township hall was demolished in 1959. The blacksmith shop and the few homes disappeared without a trace and the store was moved to Wiarton. Today only the empty church and school guard the intersection, their windows dark and vacant. As a centennial project the township erected a cairn on the site of the township hall to commemorate John Gillies and the other pioneers of Gillies Hill.

GLAMMIS

Boarded-up stores and shuttered houses cluster around the main intersection of Glammis, a partial ghost town on the flat pasture lands of
Bruce County. Twenty kilometers (12 miles) east of Kincardine, it was
once one of the county's leading towns. That was a century ago.

In 1852 the fertile farmlands of Bruce County were finally offered to
settlers. At the conjunction of three townships a group of Scottish immigrants arrived and began to clear the forests. By 1858 there were enough
Scots Presbyterians to build the first church, a small log chapel near the
crude trail that passed for a road. A few years later James Crawford
arrived and opened a general store and brought the area its first post
office. The name was inevitably Scottish, Glammis, after Glamis Castle
in Forfarshire, Scotland.

Slowly the roads improved. As settlement progressed Glammis mushroomed into a busy service town. By 1895 it contained 225 people and
more than a dozen businesses. Among them were cabinet makers, car-
penters, tinsmiths, wagonmakers, shoemakers, a sawmill and two general
stores. Benjamin McLennan operated one of the blacksmith shops, Rich-
ard Harrison a general store and the post office. Alex and Thomas Pick-
ard ran the cheese factory with boxes made on the premises. Duncan
Smith kept the popular hotel, a busy spot when the farmers were in
town. Methodists and Anglicans built churches, while Reverend John
McKinnon led the Baptist worship.

The townspeople of Glammis entered the new century full of optimism
for the future of their town. But as those early years progressed, decline
set in. Shortly before the First World War rural mail delivery replaced
the post office and fewer customers visited the general store. The railways had bypassed Glammis and any new businesses which opened in
the area did so at railway towns such as Walkerton or Hanover. Then,
after the war, a migration, slow but steady, began from the townships
and farms around Glammis to the cities of the south and east. The large
furniture factories of Hanover, Walkerton and Kincardine drove the
Glammis cabinet makers out of business just as the coming of the tractor
and automobile made its blacksmiths obsolete. Roads were improved and
the larger towns were suddenly accessible. As area residents shunned
local stores for the larger facilities, Glammis' businesses fell silent. As
they did the population fell below 100.

Today Glammis is a photogenic semi-ghost town. Because there are

Glammis is a partial ghost town with several empty stores and houses clustered around its main intersection.

those who enjoy the quiet of country living, several Glammis houses remain occupied and a few new homes have been added. However, around the intersection and along the once-busy main street, stores, garages, an implement dealer and a couple of houses stand empty. In many other rural Ontario villages which met a similar fate, empty buildings were demolished, but in Glammis they still stand and present a ghostly appearance.

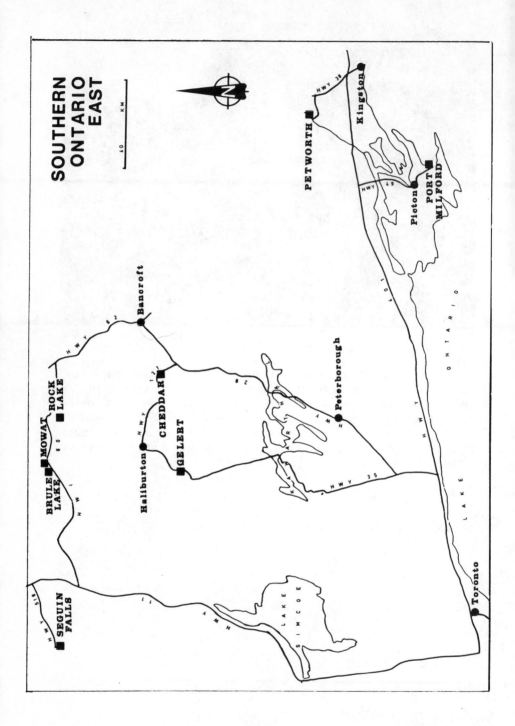

SOUTHERN ONTARIO EAST

KM

40

N

PETWORTH

Kingston

HWY 38

PORT MILFORD

Picton

HWY 49

HWY 401

Bancroft

HWY 62

MOWAT

ROCK LAKE

HWY 60

BRULE LAKE

HWY 11

CHEDDAR

HWY 121

GELERT

Haliburton

HWY 28

Peterborough

HWY 7

KAWARTHA LAKES

HWY 35

ONTARIO LAKE

SEGUIN FALLS

HWY 518

HWY 11

LAKE SIMCOE

Toronto

PORT MILFORD

Atop a small limestone bluff a few buildings and foundations overlook the sparkling waters of South Bay. They are all that remain of one of Prince Edward County's busiest ports. Port Milford at first was just one of more than a dozen barley ports which sprang up around Prince Edward's shores, but because it was sheltered by the headlands of South Bay, it boomed into a ship-building and exporting centre.

Port Milford began in the 1860s when a lone hiker arrived from Kingston, his possessions jammed into a pack. James Cooper and later his brother William, made their way south from Picton 16 kilometers (10 miles) to an attractive bay on the southeast shore of the county. At that time American distilleries had begun to import large quantities of cheap Canadian barley. Inspired by the barley boom the Cooper brothers constructed docks, stone warehouses and a general store and the village of Port Milford was born. When Earl Collier arrived, Cooper built him a fine red-brick house which stands to this day. (Collier later operated the general store). A short distance along the shore, A. W. Minaker opened a store, hotel and wharf, but by the 1880s Cooper owned this as well.

As trade grew, more ships were needed and an active ship-building industry developed. George Dixon launched the schooner *W.R. Taylor* in 1877 and the McMurchy brothers the *Huron*. Fourteen others were launched at Cooper's wharf including the *Jennie Lind, Jessie Brown, Marysburg, C. J. Collier, C. Gearing* and *Speadwell*. With the wind billowing in their sails they glided across the lakes to American ports like Rochester.

The general store is one of Port Milford's few surviving buildings.

27

James Cooper, the man who launched Port Milford, sits amid the construction work for his wharf. In this picture he is wearing a top hat and looking every bit the entrepreneur, yet when he arrived at the site of Port Milford he carried all his possessions in a knapsack.

Yet the government built no lighthouse in this busy bay. These ships had to find their way to safe harbour with the help of only a lantern on a pole. One ship which didn't make it was the *Fleetwood*. Its rotting ribs lie in the offshore waters of the bay.

In addition to barley, Port Milford shipped butter, cheese, lumber and apples. It became so busy it required a customs officer, two wharfingers and a telegraph office.

Although Port Milford's facilities could handle the smaller schooners popular in the mid-1800s, they were too small for the larger and faster steamers. With the coming of the railway in the 1880s Picton, with its deeper harbour, soon became the major, and almost exclusive, port town. The final blow came in 1890. In a nationalistic fervour U. S. President James McKinlay placed a stiff tariff on imported barley. One by one the barley wharves fell silent.

By 1900, when Port Milford's shipping days had ended, the village turned its attention inland. Since Prince Edward County's farmers had by then become a major producer of vegetables, the Church brothers selected Port Milford as a site for a large cannery. By the 1930s Canadian Canners operated the plant and Port Milford reached a size unsurpassed even in its heyday as a port. Its population shot up to 100 and along its two main streets stood nearly two dozen buildings plus the store, church and school. In the late 1930s the cannery closed and Port Milford was abandoned. Today a massive stone foundation marks the site of the cannery, while the foundations of the houses that lined the road leading to it have degenerated into grassy mounds. A half kilometer east are the foundations of Cooper's stone warehouses and the piles of lumber that were his wharves. On the bank above the wharf Earl Collier's fine brick house still stands, opposite it the vacant general store. A couple of kilometers to the west at the head of South Bay there stands a new and appropriate attraction—a mariners' museum. It houses a fine display of marine artifacts and their sagas. On the grounds is the False Ducks lighthouse. Constructed in 1832, it helped guide schooners through shoal-ridden waters into the safety of South Bay while the wharf at Port Milford made do with a pole and lantern.

PETWORTH

The Napanee River starts in swamp and rock 80 kilometers (48 miles) north of Kingston. As it sweeps southwestward it gains speed and size, conditions ideal for early mills. Along it grew a string of bustling mill towns with names like Colebrook, Yarker, Camden and Newburgh and at its mouth on Lake Ontario, Napanee. Although most of the mills are gone these villages remain as residential hamlets with attractive century-old buildings of stone. There is one, however, which grew into a sizeable village, but has now dwindled and nearly died. Most of its buildings are now empty shells. That village is Petworth.

During the 1840s settlement began to push inland from the lake and up the Napanee River. Wherever there was water power there was soon a sawmill. At one such site 25 kilometers (15 miles) upstream from Napanee there were two. One was opened in 1840 by James Foster, the other operated by one Chambers who gave the site its first name, Chambers Mills.

Exploitation of the forest accelerated. In 1845 the lumber company of Stevenson and Lott acquired extensive limits in the area and bought Foster's mill. They added a woollen mill, a carding mill for cleansing and combing the wool before spinning and a three-storey stone gristmill. Eventually the Rathbun Lumber Company took over S and L's lumbering rights and used the village to stock logs for the frantic spring log drives.

Farming was also gaining a foothold in the area. Although much of the terrain was bare rock, pockets of good soil nestled between the outcrops. Many farmers raised sheep and drove them right into town to wash them in preparation for shearing. Others, in response to the booming grain trade, hauled their sacks of grain to the gristmill. Inevitably the place soon acquired other businesses and functions needed by the rural community. Sid Peters added a blacksmith shop, Frank Gerow a cheese factory. The general stores were operated by the Van Luven brothers and James Wallace, the first postmaster, who called the place Petworth. By 1892 the village had added two churches, a school and an Orange Hall. Two hotels opened on the main street and each spring they became home to the rowdy loggers on their way downstream.

Growth and prosperity did not last long. The railway which had crept promisingly upstream, swung eastward before it reached Petworth. By 1905, when the land was clear and the timber gone, the river drives ended. Many of the marginal farms were abandoned and then, one by one, the mills and shops closed. The hotels and cheese factory burned

Several empty buildings line Petworth's main street, while others have been renovated and are still in use. This one-time blacksmith shop lies in ruin.

down. One of the churches was ignobly torn down and its lumber used elsewhere, probably for a barn.

Although Petworth has returned to life with the building of three new country homes, about half of its buildings lie empty and weathered.

Along Memorial Street, three houses, a barn and the blacksmith shop gaze forlornly onto the dirt road. On the valley rim to the east sit the old school and another old house. In their midst a few original homes remain in use. Beside the rusting iron bridge which has spanned the tumbling river for 75 years stand the walls of the Stevenson and Lott gristmill. Once the lifeblood of the quiet village, they now peer silently from the bushes that will soon overtake them.

Petworth lies 40 kilometers (24 miles) northwest of Kingston near County Road 5 off Highway 38.

CHEDDAR

During the 1850s the government of Canada West opened to settlers the wilds of northern Peterborough and southern Haliburton Counties.

From a village called Burleigh 30 kilometers (18 miles) northeast of the town of Peterborough contractors cleared and ditched the Burleigh Road. Sixty kilometers (36 miles) from where it began it met the Monck Road, an east-west colonization road and stopped. Here the junction village of Cheddar served the scattered population for as long as the rocky farms lasted. Today its houses lie collapsing in a young forest.

By 1870 both the Monck and Burleigh Roads had been made "passable". At least that is how the government described them. It still took a stagecoach half a day to travel ten kilometers (6 miles) over the logs and through the mudholes that plagued the first road. Wayside inns hurriedly constructed of logs welcomed weary wayfarers with warmth, rest, food and a soft seat after the stagecoach's hard wooden benches. It was at the important junction of the Burleigh and Monck Roads that Benjamin Woods opened a general store, post office and offered "entertainment to the travelling public" in 1871.

Woods had been born in Lincolnshire, England in 1828 and was just 24 when he migrated to Brantford, Canada West. In 1866, lured by the free land which lined the new colonization roads into the unconquered wilds, he opened his store and hotel in remote Haliburton County.

Unlike much of the land along the colonization roads the junction of the Burleigh and the Monck had pockets of stoney but tillable soil. Woods Corners, as it was known, became the focus for the scattered farmers. Besides Woods' store and hotel, James McIlven opened a blacksmith shop, while nearby Lamb and Bates operated sawmills. The hamlet soon added Methodist and Anglican churches and a school. Around 1890, A. Southwood opened a rival general store and managed to land the post office contract. When the post office opened, Southwood promptly changed the name of the village from Woods Corners to Cheddar after a town in England.

While Cheddar, England was famous for its cheese, Cheddar, Ontario became mildly famous for its uranium. W.M. Richardson first uncovered the valuable uranium in the rocky ridges northwest of Cheddar. The Ontario Radium Corporation built a 150-ton mill and operated the property from 1929 to 1931. When that operation failed, the company turned its attention to Cheddar. A kilometer south of Woods' old hamlet, uranium lurked in the rocks. For ten years, from 1932 to 1942, Canada Radium Corporation hammered and banged into the hard rocks. It built a few residences, a company store and a 100-ton mill. Then in 1942, after a few test runs proved the deposit to be uneconomical, the company closed shop and left.

Life in Cheddar offered little in the way of recreation. During the long winter the men would form a hockey team and challenge their larger

Cheddar's old boarding house is in better condition than most of its other structures which are shells sagging in the woods.

neighbours such as Wilberforce, a busy lumber town located 20 kilometers (12 miles) to the northwest. Old-timers still have vivid memories of dances where Archie Sweet set feet tapping with his lively fiddling.

By 1950 the tunes had become an echo, for Cheddar was in decline. The mines had closed and area farmers, realizing that the stoney soils were good for little but sore backs, moved away. At the same time, however, a fresh wave of seasonal settlers arrived in Haliburton. New wealth and new roads had combined to create a growing demand for lakeshore cottages. Haliburton abounded in lakes and the boom was on. The old twisting gravel trails that were the Burleigh and Monck Roads were paved and straightened to bypass Cheddar. Suddenly the once strategic junction was no better than a backwater.

Today, Cheddar lies totally abandoned. A sign on Highway 121, 37 kilometers (22 miles) east of Haliburton village still announces the "Cheddar Road" but it is barely passable. The woods have reclaimed both the mine and Woods Corners and the buildings sag behind maple saplings. Only the one-time boarding house remains solid. Although its name still appears on maps, Cheddar is a village of the past.

As Cheddar died the uranium rush continued. Companies like Bicroft and Faraday discovered valuable deposits and built their own towns. In less than ten years the mines produced 11-million pounds of uranium valued at $105 million. Today, although the mines have closed and their sites are out of bounds to visitors, the townsites still exist a few kilometers east of Cheddar.

GELERT

The Haliburton Highlands today are a recreational mecca. Once attractive lakes are now ringed with a wall of cottages that resemble the suburbs the cottagers flee. But a century ago the area was a part of the new Ontario, a place for farmers to clear the forests and till the unbroken soils. As railways wound through its valleys, villages appeared at railside to ship lumber and cattle. With the closing of the railways, the razing of the forests and the abandonment of the farms, many settlements dwindled only to resurface as recreational towns. But those in the valleys away from the lakes never recovered. The half-abandoned village of Gelert is one of these.

Until the 1850s the Haliburton Highlands remained inaccessible. Its small lakes and shallow rivers were its only highways. During that decade, to open this wilderness, the government of Canada West devised its colonization road scheme. To provide the influential lumber companies with food and labour the government attracted pioneer settlers with offers of free land.

By 1860 the Bobcaygeon Road had been surveyed northward from the Kawartha Lakes. Although much of the land through which it passed was rock and swamp, it did open pockets of level, sandy soil and these quickly sprouted bustling pioneer communities.

Gelert was located on a branch road which linked Kinmount on the Bobcaygeon Road with Haliburton on the Buckhorn Road. At first it was only a rural community with a sawmill, church and store known as "Little Ireland".

When Gelert was a busy railway shipping town, this stagecoach picked up passengers at the boarding houses and offered them a bumpy ride to nearby Minden.

The Gelert side street that led to the railway siding is now a row of empty shells.

The arrival of the Victoria Railway in 1880 changed all that. Overnight "Little Ireland" boomed into a busy shipping town. By 1895 it contained wool, shingle and saw mills and Methodist and Anglican churches. A side street was surveyed from the road to the siding and along it appeared Clark's blacksmith, Connors' hotel and Dawson's and Ritchie's general stores. Hartle and Levis operated a busy stage line shuttling passengers and freight between Gelert and the growing mill town of Minden eight kilometers (5 miles) northwest on the Gull River. Most of the new arrivals were English and the old name was quickly replaced with "Gelert".

Development also changed methods of construction. Like most of Haliburton's pioneer communities Gelert's first church and school were made with logs. These were soon replaced by frame buildings.

The peak of Gelert's prosperity was short. The soils which were productive at first were quickly depleted. In the first decade of this century alone, nearly two dozen farms were deserted. Fires from careless lumbering razed what remained of the forests. The siding was lifted and Gelert lost its economic mainstay, shipping.

For several years the store continued to serve a shrinking rural community and eventually even it closed down. Finally, in 1980 the CNR closed the little-used branch line completely.

Today Gelert is a semi-ghost town. Fewer than half its buildings are in use, the rest lie vacant and weathering. Stores and houses on the side street sit idle, while in the grass beside the now silent track there is little evidence of the busy cattle and lumber shipping that once took place here.

The Haliburton-Kinmount Road has been upgraded to a secondary highway, but it leads to few lakes and is only lightly travelled by cottagers. Those who do are passing the ghosts of another era when they pass through Gelert.

SECTION TWO

COTTAGE COUNTRY

Countless islands and quiet coves mark the shores of Georgian Bay and northern Lake Huron. Along this indented shoreline and its hinterland, during the latter years of the 19th century, there appeared smoky sawmill towns, bustling summer fishing villages and even a few mining towns. While the fish and forests lasted, these settlements boomed. However, careless exploitation exhausted the resources after only a few decades and the towns died, creating the ghost towns of Ontario's cottage country.

Before the white settlers arrived, the Georgian Bay, its islands, forested shores and powerful rivers were home to the Ojibway and the fur traders. Indians and voyageurs guided their fur-laden canoes down the wide windy North Channel that separates Manitoulin Island from Lake Huron's north shore. They would venture into the maze of channels that marks the mouth of the French River of wind their way through the Thirty Thousand Islands that hide the eastern shore of Georgian Bay. Along these waters the French and later the British built a dozen fur trading posts. Even as settlers flocked to southern Ontario this area remained largely unsettled. But when the Toronto Northern Railway was completed to Collingwood on southern Georgian Bay in 1855 a dramatic change took place. Almost overnight the railway brought the southern cities with their growing demand for lumber within reach of the Georgian Bay pine. The first mills appeared in the southeastern corner of the Bay. Later, mills were built further up the Thirty Thousand Islands and across the north shore of Lake Huron.

The railways also transformed the fishing industry. To meet the new demand, fishermen from the southern Georgian Bay towns of Meaford, Collingwood and Owen Sound had to fish further afield. Eventually they began to build summer villages on larger islands near the remote fishing banks.

More railways appeared at Midland, Owen Sound and Wiarton. From these terminals steamers puffed into the Bay, providing a vital supply link for the remote shoreline towns. Then in 1898 another change took place. Because they had to pay a steep tariff on imported lumber, American lumbermen boomed their Canadian logs across to mills on the American shore. When outraged Canadians persuaded the Ontario Government to place a ban on the export of uncut logs, the Americans quickly moved their operations to the Canadian shores.

The first two decades of the 20th century were the peak years for the fishing and milling towns, but their days were to be short-lived. The

35

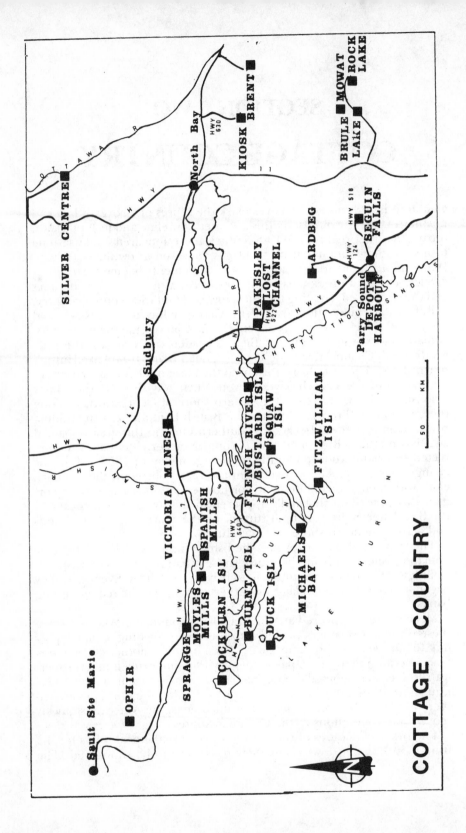

COTTAGE COUNTRY

lumbermen were careless in their practices and what forests weren't clear-cut were burned. Soon the forests were gone and by the 1930s most of the mills had burned or closed. Considerable mill waste ended up in fish spawning beds and severely cut the stock of whitefish and lake trout. By the 1930s the deadly lamprey eel had made its way into the Great Lakes from the ocean and killed most of the remaining fish. By 1950 the fishing industry was nearly dead. By then the advent of diesel tugs had led to the abandonment of most of the summer fishing villages. Those that were not revived as summer cottages were left marooned and are gradually being obliterated by the relentless whittling of the wind and the waves.

The ghost towns of cottage country are largely abandoned and many retain the ghostly reminders of their early days. While some of the sawmill and fishing villages have vanished with little trace, others have several buildings, though badly weathered, still in place. Several sites have become popular cottage spots and a number of their buildings are kept up for seasonal use.

MOWAT

Algonquin Park today is a contradiction. The Ontario government, its manager, calls it a wilderness while still permitting noisy and sometimes careless lumbering practices. The Algonquin Park of yesterday made no pretence at wilderness. It was an unquestionable timber reserve for the exclusive use of such influential lumber kings as J. R. Booth and the Gilmour brothers.

A network of rail lines penetrated the pine stands to reap the wooden bounty. The Ottawa, Arnprior and Parry Sound, nicknamed the "Booth Line", was the first. Opened in 1897 it was a part of John Rudolphus Booth's empire and was designed largely to carry his logs to his Ottawa mills. It was also designed to provide the shortest route from the growing cities of the upper lakes to Montreal and the Atlantic ocean ports. Its Georgian Bay terminus of Depot Harbour rivalled all Great Lakes' ports for three decades. The second was the Canadian Northern Railway which opened the northeastern corner of the park in 1914. From each main line, short spur lines stabbed into the forests to haul logs to the railside mills. Around these mills grew the mill towns, some little more than bunks and a cookery, while others contained stores, schools, churches and homes.

The Gilmour brothers made Canoe Lake a virtual pond for their Mowat mill after they discovered they couldn't get logs to their mill in Trenton without them rotting.

Following the demise of the Gilmour mills, Mowat was resurrected as a popular tourist destination. While a guest at the lodge, the famous Canadian artist Tom Thomson drowned in a mysterious canoeing accident.

Mowat, one of the largest, was born out of failure. The Gilmour brothers owned the limits but their mills lay in Trenton on Lake Ontario. To transport their logs they had to conquer 325 kilometers (200 miles) of lakes, swamp and rocks. Despite an ingenious system of river drives and complicated portages, the journey took two seasons to complete.

From Canoe Lake the Gilmours boomed their logs down the Oxtongue River to Lake of Bays, a lake familiar to Toronto cottagers. From the east end of that lake a great spiked chain dragged the logs up a high flume from the top of which they glided down a mile-long trough to a second chain and a second trough which flushed them into Raven Lake and on into the Kawartha Lakes. From there the logs shunted down the Trent River to their final destination of the Gilmour mills at Trenton. By the time they reached the mills, even the best logs had begun to rot. Needless to say, the Gilmours were desperately searching for a mill site closer to their limits.

Booth's line offered that opportunity. In 1896 the Department of Lands and Forests granted the brothers a ten-year licence "for the purpose of erecting a saw and planing mill together with the necessary buildings and houses to be used in connection therewith... (they) shall properly survey and lay out lots and streets on which it is proper to construct workmen's houses... All buildings shall be of good construction and when made of boards they shall be painted or whitewashed."

The town would be called Mowat and was located at the narrow north end of Canoe Lake. The rocky shoreline defied a street pattern and most buildings hugged the water. At the mouth of Potter Creek loomed the large mill and nearby the boarding house and the grand homes of the

John Rudolpus Booth, Ontario's 19th century lumber king inspects a trainload
of lumber before it departs his Algonquin Park limits.

managers and the Gilmours themselves. A log bridge crossed the creek to a peninsula where most of the workers' cabins stood.

A kilometer north stood the Canoe Lake station with its water tower, pump house and divisional quarters. Between the two lay 18 kilometers (11 miles) of siding. In the first years the Gilmours turned Canoe Lake into a private mill pond, the sea of logs stretching as far as the eye could see. During this period Mowat's population soared to 700, making it the largest permanent community ever to exist within Algonquin Park.

Working conditions were among the best. With wages elsewhere at 50 cents to $1 per day, the Gilmours paid their workers $1.50. When the residents petitioned for a school, the company provided the lumber for its construction while the Department of Education donated half of the teacher's $200 salary. Later the town acquired a Presbyterian mission church and a post office.

The town led a prosperous but brief existence. By 1900 the Gilmours were bankrupt. To facilitate their liquidation the Department of Lands and Forests extended their licence of occupation to 1911 while the Gilmours sold or salvaged what they could. From 1909 to 1912 they leased several of their buildings to the Huntsville Lumber Company but the company was beyond recovery. By 1912 the lake, the bay and the town stood empty and silent.

By 1913 tourists had discovered Algonquin Park. Lumbering had declined and resorts began to appear on those lakes which were close to the railway. Lying in the path of the tourism wave, Mowat's buildings did not remain empty for long. Cottagers moved into some of the larger houses while the Shannon Frasers, hired by the Gilmour receivers to supervise the property, converted the old boarding house into a resort— Mowat Lodge.

The Omanique Lumber Company erected a mill at Mowat long after the Gilmours had departed.

41

One lodge guest was Canadian artist Tom Thomson, who quickly became a favourite of the Fraser family. He stayed at the lodge many times and made trips to the park during the winter, staying at the lodge while it was closed to tourists. The natural beauty of Algonquin Park was the inspiration for many of his well-known works. Canoe Lake was also the sight of his mysterious and untimely death. On July 8, 1917 he failed to return from a fishing trip. His canoe was found later that day, floating empty in the lake. His body was recovered a week later, but the mystery of his death has never been solved. How did an experienced paddler and woodsman drown on placid Canoe Lake? The reasons given range from the most trivial—he snagged himself on his own fishing line— to the most sinister—murder. No one knows what pulled him into the lake that day.

Following a fire in 1930 the Frasers moved away and Mowat Lodge passed into history. For a time during the 1920s and 30s the Canoe Lake Lumber Company and the Omanique Lumber Company opened new mills on Potter Creek but the village never attained its former size or activity. By 1940 a bridge washout had severed Booth's line and the mills creaked to a halt.

Some of Mowat has survived. The two large Gilmour homes are used as cottages, although when the leases expire they will be demolished. The mill foundations and an old stone fireplace poke from a grassy field by the shore. Nearby the cribbing from the dock is still visible and the log bridge still rambles across the creek to the peninsula. The simpler cabins, hospital, school and stables have all disappeared into a young forest.

A part of the village of Rock Lake in the 1920s. The new station is the light-roofed building at the right.

ROCK LAKE was another busy Park village on the Booth Line. Located near the Park's eastern boundary it became the headquarters for the McCrea Lumber Company mill on Lake of Two Rivers. In the 30s the mill moved to Whitney outside the Park and then in 1942 moved back to Rock Lake where it operated until 1978. It was finally demolished in 1982. Rock Lake was also a divisional point on the Booth Line railway and after the central portion was abandoned in 1933, became its western terminus. Its water tower, station and several railway houses all served as landmarks until the entire railway was abandoned and they were demolished.

One of the most impressive Rock Lake houses was the Barclay estate. Owned by J.R. Booth's son-in-law, it was a summer retreat and boasted tennis courts, large servants' quarters and several acres of landscaped grounds. Sadly, an offer by the owners to donate the historic mansion to the Ontario government for use as a children's convalescent hospital was rejected and the building was demolished. The site today is a lovely small campground which stretches out into the lake on a point of land. Tents are now pitched on the broad landscaped grounds.

The third of Algonquin Park's Booth Line lumber towns was **BRULE LAKE.** It lay a few kilometers west of Canoe Lake, close to the western boundary of the Park.

Records are conflicting as to who built Brule Lake's first mill. Directories of the day list P. S. Duff Ltd. as the mill-owner in 1905, while the *Canadian Lumberman and Woodworker*, a lumber magazine, has A. Barnet in charge.

At Brule Lake piles of lumber stretched for a mile along the railway siding awaiting shipment. At times the piles extended almost to the next lake.

Brule Lake was a busy Algonquin Park mill village when the Duff mills were operating. Many of these buildings survived until the 1950s when the then Department of Lands and Forests burned them.

Visitors in 1905 described Brule Lake as a "lumber settlement and post office" with "good fishing and good hunting".

Twenty-three buildings randomly dotted the beach or perched on the rocky cliffs. Besides the mill and its accessory buildings were Barnet's boarding house, a one-room frame school, a store, a busy 24-hour railway station and large wooden homes belonging to the Christies, Cousineaus and Gervais while smaller cabins housed mill workers and their families. Piles of sawn lumber awaiting shipment often stretched a kilometer along the track.

Activities at Brule Lake changed with each season. Winter was a busy time in the camps on Browns Lake where the lumberjacks prepared the timber for its spring drive.

During the summer the mill roared into life and cut sawlogs for market. The fall season witnessed an influx of hunters to stalk the deer in Algonquin Park's remaining woodlands.

In 1927 Peter Duff moved back to Brule Lake and stayed until 1943 when the Muskoka Wood Company acquired the mill. When the mill burned in 1950 Muskoka Wood, rather than rebuild, trucked the logs to its Huntsville mill. Most of the Brule Lake workers followed and the village soon stood empty. Then in 1952 the village of Brule Lake vanished from the earth when the Department of Lands and Forests burned the remaining buildings.

In 1959 the tracks were lifted and the last vestige of Booth's railway vanished. Brule Lake is now a field of rubble, its one-time huge lumberyard a clearing by the cindered roadbed. The town survives only in photographs housed in the Park museum and in the memories of the old loggers who once called Brule Lake home.

SEGUIN FALLS

Sixty kilometers (37 miles) west of Algonquin Park two once-promising transportation lines intersect: the heralded railway built by lumber millionaire J. R. Booth and Peter Vankoughnet's Rosseau-Nipissing Colonization Road. Both began with loud fanfare; both ultimately failed. As part of the Ontario government's effort to settle central Ontario, the Nipissing Road was completed in 1875 from Lake Rosseau to Lake Nipissing. Its 100 kilometers (60 miles) traversed some of Ontario's worst farmland, the few pockets of soil were sandy and infertile. However, buoyed by glowing government propaganda, settlers swarmed along the road to carve farmsteads from the forests. To serve the needs of the pioneer, stores, sawmills and hotels appeared and became the focus for a string of villages.

Seguin Falls began as a camp for road workers. Located at the junction with the Christie colonization road, the intersection became a busy stagecoach stop. To accommodate travellers bone-weary from a jolting half-day's stage journey through potholes and over corduroy roads, D. F. Burk erected a simple wooden hotel and Adam Fitzer a store. The site took the name Seguin Falls and soon added a school, while a few lots south, William Eastway donated land for the first church.

"The traveller will find an excellent temperance hotel," wrote one visitor in 1873, "the proprietor of which Mr. D. F. Burk is a most genial and hospitable host." Almost as an afterthought he added "nor should

A rare old gas pump sits disused in front of the Seguin Falls hotel, which was known for its fine food... and the fact that beer and liquor were not available.

45

The Nipissing Road is Seguin Falls' "main street".

we forget to praise the excellent cuisine of his good lady." Still further south where the road crossed a small tributary of the Seguin River, James Critz ran a sawmill to supply material for the building boom and opened a hotel to rival Burk's. Between the two hotels and along the Christie Road were 13 farmsteads freshly cut from the wilderness.

Then in 1897 a shrill steam whistle pierced the air. Crossing the road two kilometers south of the village, belching smoke, was the inaugural train of the Booth Line railway. The faster, more comfortable railway replaced the slow stagecoach and quickly drew Seguin Falls' businesses away from the old intersection. The Spence Lumber Company erected a saw and shingle mill adjacent to the station and the Nipissing Road became the main street to a brand new village. Within a few years the new Seguin Falls could boast a frame church and brick school, the King George Hotel, two general stores and post office and a string of houses. Larger homes sat serenely in the shade of a maple-lined avenue south of the station while north of the station, simple labourers' cabins perched randomly on the rocky hilltops.

Records are sketchy as to how many people called Seguin Falls home or even how many homes there were. A local resident estimates a peak population of 500 while aerial photographs reveal the foundations or shells of at least 20 houses.

After the mill closed, its timber supply exhausted, a slow decline began. This was hastened when, in 1933, this portion of the Booth Line was abandoned and a few years later the station dismantled. Farmers gradually gave up on the land and by 1956, the last year of the post office, the general store was serving fewer than a dozen regular customers.

Today, of the 12 buildings which still stand, most are vacant. Some are used seasonally, among them a weathered wooden mansion, the King George hotel and the school. The mill, station and church have barely any foundations left, while under the maples and on the hilltops the shells of the houses and cabins shakily await collapse. Ontario's Ministry of Natural Resources maintains Booth's railway roadbed as a snowmobile trail while the Nipissing Road is passable up to three kilometers south of the village. Beyond that it is best left to jeeps or hikers.

The site lies three kilometers (4.8 miles) south of Highway 532 east of the town of Parry Sound. This collection of old buildings on a dead-end wilderness trail is a striking discovery.

46

DEPOT HARBOUR

John Rudolphus Booth was Ontario's most prominent 19th century lumber baron. He alone built a railway and indirectly created a string of towns and villages that dotted the highlands between Ottawa and Georgian Bay. Born of an Irish farmer on the Yamaska River in Quebec, Booth moved with his family to Ottawa (then called Bytown) in 1852. After a few years as sawmill manager on Leamy's Lake in Quebec, Booth foresaw a booming sawmill industry. In 1858 he leased a sawmill and a year later underbid the Ottawa Valley's established lumbermen to obtain the cherished contract to construct Ottawa's first parliament buildings. Just eight years later a block of prized timberland went up for auction. Armed with first-hand reports of the unusually high quality of its pine, Booth outbid the more cautious established lumbermen and obtained the best timber in the Ottawa Valley. It was the beginning of his empire and there was no looking back.

His biggest undertaking was the Canada Atlantic Railway. In 1879, he acquired a financially troubled and partially completed railway in Vermont. By 1883 he had completed the line and suddenly had rail access from his Ottawa mills to the ice-free Atlantic ports, an advantage other Ottawa lumbermen lacked. Then in 1894, to tap the growing Great Lakes' grain trade, he extended his line across the height of land from Ottawa to Georgian Bay and could then offer grain shippers the shortest route to the Atlantic.

A string of villages grew at key points along the railway. Some died and are the subject of stories in Ontario's ghost town annals. Others have survived and contain unusual relics of the Booth railway era. East of Algonquin Park in a village called Madawaska, stands a grey shell of a massive railway roundhouse. Further east is Barry's Bay containing the best preserved station and only water tower on the old Booth Line. The most remarkable of all these towns was Depot Harbour, the western terminus of the Canada Atlantic Railway. Perhaps more than any other single accomplishment, the building and development of Depot Harbour typified Booth's ambition and ingenuity.

After acquiring extensive timber limits in Algonquin Park and having pushed his Canada Atlantic Railway from Ottawa to Georgian Bay in the hope of intercepting the lucrative grain trade, Booth realized all he needed was a harbour and labour. The town of Parry Sound had both, but landowners there overpriced their properties, at least in Booth's eyes, and the impecunious lumber king looked elsewhere.

He found exactly what he wanted seven kilometers (4 miles) away on the Parry Island Indian Reserve. On the island, sheltered from the wind and waves, was a natural harbour that was deep and clear. A flat sandy backshore supplied a terrain that was ideal for shipping facilities and a townsite. He laid out a 12-block town plan and in 1897 Depot Harbour

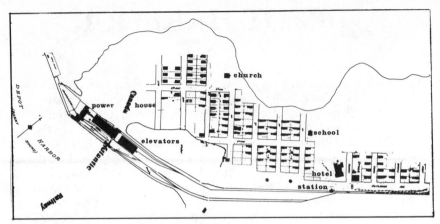

Town plan and layout for Depot Harbour.

Depot Harbour once claimed nearly 100 houses on its 12 city blocks and in the first 20 years of this century rivalled other Georgian Bay ports such as Midland and Collingwood.

was born. His construction crew went to work and almost overnight streets boasted stores, a railway office, station, a three-storey hotel and 89 single and duplex dwellings. Docking facilities included a coal dock, warehouses and a one-million-ton grain elevator. The railway facilities included several miles of sidings and a large roundhouse. There was piped water, electricity, fire hydrants and cement sidewalks. Along the streets Booth planted maple saplings.

Suddenly Depot Harbour and J.R. Booth's railway provided the upper Great Lakes' shippers with the shortest route to the important ocean port of Montreal and even to the Atlantic ports. Older port towns like Collingwood, Midland and Owen Sound saw their trade drift to this upstart town. Booth doubled the capacity of the grain elevators and trains puffed in and out every 20 minutes.

As the town expanded it became one of Canada's destinations for European immigrants and numbered among its population 11 different ethnic groups.

By 1911 the population had soared to 600, a few years later to 1,500. They joined in Saturday night dances held in the general store, jeered at each other in a vigorous pool game or simply skated leisurely around the town rink. Children attended classes in a two-storey frame public school; their families worshipped in the Anglican, Presbyterian or Roman Catholic churches.

The tranquillity of the town may have been in part due to Booth's ban on booze. As if to further frustrate human thirst, William Beatty had imposed a similar prohibition on Parry Sound. However, thirsty lumbermen and railway workers are not easily outdone and on the bank of the Seguin River opposite Parry Sound, beyond the bans of both Beatty and Booth, arose Parry Harbour, a boisterous backwater of bars and brothels. It easily earned its nickname, "Parry Hoot".

Parry Hoot was intended as the original terminus of the Parry Sound colonization road from Bracebridge. A townsite was surveyed and given the name Codrington. However, it was quickly surpassed by William Beatty's newer mill town Parry Sound and, free of Beatty's prohibition on liquor, quickly became the area's recreational outlet. Taverns sprouted on town lots and a shack town sprang up on the steep barren rocklands that surround it. Loggers, fishermen and railwaymen crowded into its pubs. Today the village is a Parry Sound suburb. Small modern bungalows have replaced the first shanties, while empty stores and former taverns still occupy the commercial square. One of the area's oldest hotels, the Kipling continues to dominate the heart of the village and is still a popular tavern.

For three decades Depot Harbour boomed. However, in 1928 a series of events began which were gradually to turn the promising port into a ghost town. In that year Canadian National Railway, having purchased the Canada Atlantic Railway four years earlier, decided to centralize its facilities. It shut down the roundhouse and office and moved the shops to South Parry on its own main line. Most of the workers followed. Just five years later in the spring of 1933, the Cache Two Rivers railway trestle

The burning of Depot Harbour's grain elevators in celebration of the end of World War 2 hastened the demise of the once promising grain port.

in Algonquin Park was so weakened by an ice jam that even a small train could not pass safely. Unexpectedly, the federal government, facing a depression, refused the CNR the funds necessary to repair the bridge, a decision that eliminated through-train traffic. Suddenly, Depot Harbour no longer provided the shortest grain route to the ocean. It had lost its main reason for existence.

As the depression deepened, the elevators remained empty and the townspeople moved away. So many houses sat vacant that one of the two water towers collapsed from disuse.

Then the dark days of World War Two descended. Ten kilometers (six miles) across the bay at Nobel, Canadian Industries Limited manufactured explosives. A key ingredient in the process was cordite. While the few remaining Depot Harbour residents commuted across the water to Nobel, C.I.L. stored the volatile cordite in the empty grain elevators. When the war ended and V-J day was celebrated most of it was still in the elevator. Late that night, into the black Georgian Bay sky, there suddenly shot a ball of flame so bright that surprised Parry Sounders seven kilometers (4.2 miles) away claimed they could read by it. In the sober morning light the torched elevators were steaming charred rubble.

The town continued to hang on by a thread. Following the war occasional trains chugged in to transship coal and ore pellets. When CNR planked in its short swing-bridge to the mainland, Depot Harbour residents moved to the better facilities at Parry Sound. They would drive across to the few jobs left at the port just as you can do today. After five decades, its houses now empty, the little harbour finally fell silent. The railway sold the buildings for their lumber value and weeds and bushes began to reclaim the roads, sidewalks and foundations. The Catholic Church survived until the 1960s when it burned. One house still stands while near the town's one-time entrance, in the shadow of a young forest, there lurks the arching walls of the railway roundhouse.

The maples which Booth planted are now mature. However they line sidewalks that are cracked and heaved, offering shade only to weedy crumbling foundations and lonely overgrown streets.

COCKBURN ISLAND

Cockburn Island is unique. It is the only ghost town in Ontario which still elects a municipal council. Every election year a few of the former islanders brave the North Channel for the municipal vote and probably a little hunting. A 6,500-hectare (2,600-acre) limestone island four kilometers (2.5 miles) from Manitoulin's western tip, Cockburn Island had at its peak two school districts, a farming community, four villages and a population of 1,000. Now there are just two permanent residents.

In the 1870s the land rush to Manitoulin Island was in full swing. Many settlers squatted on Cockburn Island before the surveyors arrived, even before the Cockburn Island Indian band agreed to sell. When surveyor J. W. Fitzgerald arrived in 1878 he found squatters who had been there for five years—and Zebe Tolsma.

A fisherman from Cheboygan, Michigan, Tolsma wanted better access to Lake Huron's northern fishing banks. On the eastern shore of the island's only natural harbour he built Cockburn Island's first village. "He has built and opened a store, erected a large boarding house and several dwellings for the use of the men," wrote a surprised Fitzgerald in 1878. "During the season profitable employment for a large number of men is thus given in fishing, salting, packing etc. During the winter these men are partly employed in getting out and storing ice." By 1883 Tolsma's village totalled 17 buildings.

His Cockburn Island base gave him access to the prized fishing grounds of the North Channel between Manitoulin Island and the mainland. From his second base on the Duck Islands he could fish the banks south

A panorama of Tolsmaville today from approximately the site of Zebe Tolsma's pioneering fishing station.

Cockburn Island contained several pockets of productive farming lands. The Scotch Block was the island's major rural community.

of Manitoulin. However, the Cockburn Island harbour lay partly exposed[1] to the 100-kilometer (60-mile) sweep of the North Channel and the force of waves and ice destroyed Tolsma's wharf. This endless battle with nature's destructive might made a permanent island harbour a tough challenge.

In 1884 Tolsma mysteriously vanished. Although a succession of families continued the operation, Zebe Tolsma never came back.

Although much of the island is a stoney limestone plain Fitzgerald claimed that "with the exception of a narrow belt around the southwest and north shore the whole interior is fairly suited for agriculture." With that endorsement the Cockburn Island Indian Band authorized the Department of Indian Affairs to sell the land to settlers at 50 cents per acre and kept for themselves only a portion at the northwestern point. Soon, each arriving steamer unloaded settlers eager to take up their new lots. In 1881 the township was incorporated and elected its first reeve, John McPherson.

On the west side of the bay opposite Tolsma's fishing village the federal government erected a public dock and surveyed a townsite. The shore soon sprouted a church, school, town hall and community centre and became the island's administrative and social centre. It adopted the name of the Island's founder, Tolsmaville.

Meanwhile four kilometers (2.5 miles) south of Tolsmaville a small group of pioneers began to carve the island's first farms out of the thick forests. Led by the Goodmurphys, McLeods, Reids and Houghts, the Scotch Block formed the island's agricultural mainstay. Farming boomed and within 20 years the island's four concession roads contained more than 40 farms. Nevertheless, lumbering was the island's main economic activity. In 1877 the Chicago firm of Hitchcock and Foster began to strip the forests and boom the logs to its Drummond Island mills, refusing the island even a mill for local construction. In 1898 when the Ontario government prohibited the export of uncut lumber, Alex MacKenzie built Cockburn Island's first sawmill. Over the next 40 years more than six different mill operators cut Cockburn's lush forests.

In a rocky bay on the south shore of the island, Owen Sound's Lawson Brothers built the island's third village, Ricketts Harbour. Here, at the site of a former lumber camp, the Lawsons built a saw and shingle mill, store, Anglican Mission chapel, boarding house and several small wooden cabins. Nearby, the Olmsteds operated a fishing station and for several years the distant cove buzzed with the coming and going of fishing and lumber tugs. Then it fell silent.

On the northwest corner of the island stood a dozen frame and log buildings which was the Indian village of Jabaiansing. Unlike other chiefs, when Joe Wahgoush was faced with the tide of white settlement, he decided to sell it directly to the settlers rather than surrender the land to the government.

Wahgoush's band mixed well with the whites and many attended Anglican services in the Tolsmaville church. The Catholic band members built their own church on the reserve. Both Catholics and Anglicans quickly grew disenchanted with the reserve's little public school and each group pressed for its own parochial school at the Sheshegwaning Reserve on nearby Manitoulin Island. While the Catholic bishop hesitated, the Anglican bishop agreed and the band split: the Catholics remaining on Cockburn, the Anglicans moving to Sheshegwaning.

Wahgoush stayed with his shrinking band, but could do little to halt

An abandoned scow rests in the harbour at Cockburn Island.

Tolsmaville's main street is quiet now compared to the days when Cockburn Island was a busy fishing, farming and forestry centre.

the drift from the reserve. Most members gradually moved to the new reserve on Manitoulin; others went west to a reserve on Drummond Island.

To this day the Cockburn band has never surrendered its land. Published maps still show "Indian Reserve 19" but have added the words "abandoned Indian Village".

For 40 years Cockburn Island prospered. Fishermen and farmers swelled the population to over 300 and when the loggers crowded the boarding houses during the peak of the lumbering season, the population soared to 1,000. The Davis Company took over Tolsma's fishing station while the steamers *Caribou, Manitou, Normac* and *Norgoma* linked the island with dozens of other Georgian Bay communities.

The years after the first war saw the Island's first setback. Returning veterans sought better jobs and brighter lights in Ontario's towns and cities. Overfishing and the sea lamprey combined to devastate the trout fishing and drive fishermen from the waters. The Duncan McLeod family, the Island's last fishermen, wound in their nets for the final time in 1944.

By 1947 small-scale lumbering was also finished. Then, reminiscent of the early Hitchcock and Foster monopoly, the Ontario Paper Company purchased three-quarters of the Island's land area to harvest and regenerate timber. It established its own staff house, rebuilt the general store and established a hunting camp.

It didn't help; the decline accelerated. Changing farm economies dated the small island farms. While the Ontario Paper Company provided jobs for some, it used largely imported work crews. By 1951 the population slipped below 100 and by 1961 it had fallen to 66. The village school

54

closed its doors for the last time in 1961. The final death knell came two years later when the steamer *Norgoma*, black smoke belching into the sky, edged away from the wharf for the last time. Now isolated in the era of the motor car and television, Cockburn Island's remaining residents moved sadly to the north shore.

Much of Cockburn Island stands as it was left. Most of the original homes still line Tolsmaville's three streets while the hall, church and school receive occasional coats of fresh paint. The Scotch Block school also survives although most of the family farms have been reduced to their foundations.

Ricketts Harbour and Zebe Tolsma's original fishing village are now little more than piles of rotting lumber and submerged cribbings.

However, the spirit among ex-Islanders remains high. Many still make the long and often dangerous journey over the rough waters of the North Channel for summer vacations and fall hunting and continue to elect a reeve and council.

In 1981 islanders staged a reunion to celebrate the island's "centennial". Sporting period costumes, they danced, watched fireworks and reminisced about the day when the island was their home. But when the activity had subsided and the islanders departed for the mainland, Cockburn Island's empty buildings were once again left to stand silent sentinel over the memories.

To reach Cockburn Island, you must charter passage from either Meldrum Bay on Manitoulin Island or Thessalon on the north shore. It will be a trip to Ontario's only ghost township.

THE GEORGIAN BAY FISHING ISLANDS

Georgian Bay's waters are famous for their 30,000 islands. Today they are home to cottagers, campers or just a colony of gulls, although many once contained busy summer fishing villages.

As soon as the spring ice had cracked and floated out of Georgian Bay, the fishermen of Collingwood, Meaford and Owen Sound, impatient after a winter of net-mending, packed families and equipment into fishing boats and set sail for their summer fishing islands. Here, close to the fishing grounds they would pack their daily catch in ice and await the buyers' boat.

Before 1850 the Georgian Bay fishery remained small and supplied only local markets. In 1855, when Toronto Northern Railway hit Collingwood, all of southern Ontario and even the northeastern United States could quickly receive Georgian Bay's whitefish and trout—still fresh in their ice-packed crates.

More and more fishermen pushed further into the Bay until they required summer accommodation on the distant banks. Most of the fishing islands housed only one or two families. Some however, blossomed into sizeable villages. The biggest were those on the Bustard, Fitzwilliam, Duck and Squaw Islands.

After 1900, enclosed diesel tugs replaced the muscle and wind-powered mackinaws allowing the skippers to travel directly from their home ports. Then overfishing, sawmill pollution and the deadly lamprey eel combined to deplete the once-bountiful schools. By the 1930s the North Shore fishery was but a shadow of its former self. By the 1950s it was virtually dead. Tugs and skiffs were hauled out for the last time and the summer fishing villages stood empty.

FITZWILLIAM ISLAND is a large limestone ledge southeast of Manitoulin Island. In 1901, 26 families huddled around the sheltered shores of Rattlesnake Harbour, a circular indentation at the north point of the island. It was a bustling scene with wooden cabins jostling for shoreline space and rowboats crisscrossing the bay.

James Cleland Hamilton visited Fitzwilliam in 1898 and left this firsthand account. "Across the harbour nets were drying. There was a small shop, a fish-packing plant, two or three shanties then a large tent occupied by a half-breed family." In addition Hamilton observed an encampment of Manitoulin Indians who operated three of the 13 smacks (single-masted sailboats with a well for fish in the hold) in the harbour.

The busy scene soon disappeared. By the First World War only a dozen men fished there. By the Second War there were none. In 1964 only four abandoned buildings guarded the site of the former village. Today these have collapsed into piles of rotting lumber.

At the turn of the century the fishermen's village on Fitzwilliam Island was a busy spot.

Fitzwilliam's most notorious event occurred before the fishing even began. In 1828 a fierce November gale blew the *Alice Hackett* into a rock bank near the harbour entrance. The crew, staggering from effects other than the motion of the waves, braved the darkness and the storm to lug the cargo, several barrels of pork and whiskey, safely ashore. They even managed to get a nervous horse to safety. However, in their stupor they left on board a woman and her infant son. In the grey morning light an ashamed and hungover crew waded back to the vessel to retrieve the distraught passenger and her wailing son.

SQUAW ISLAND was a much larger village. When Hamilton visited it he "entered Squaw Island harbour in the shape of a horseshoe 500 yards across. The houses, the usual summer shanties are on the south side. As our boat passed in, a score of men and boys came out to meet us."

Squaw Island lies northeast of Manitoulin. Each year 60 fishermen and their families gathered from Collingwood, Lion's Head, Meaford and Killarney. "There were many nets on racks and spread on the rocks" recounted Hamilton. "Men were unrolling them, women and children were about the houses all looking happy and comfortable." According to the 1903 edition of the navigation manual *The Georgian Bay Pilot*, Squaw Island was the principal fishing station in its corner of the Bay and harboured a fleet of 50 skiffs and three tugs. In fact, it was large enough to boast a school and a Presbyterian summer mission.

As with Fitzwilliam, the decline struck in the early years of this century.

By 1916 fewer than 20 men were fishing from three tugs. Several decades later there were none.

GREAT DUCK ISLAND is the largest of a group of limestone islands known as the Ducks that lie off the southwest shores of Manitoulin. Fishing began here in the 1880s with the C. W. Gauthier Company. Its fleet of tugs included the *Walter Scott, Gordon Gauthier, H. Smith, E. K. Roberts* and the *H. Gauthier*.

At the turn of the century, with Lake Huron fishing at its peak, Great Duck Island's population approached 100. The shore of the harbour contained an ice house, packing plant, net shed, 13 houses and a semi-portable sawmill operated by Eric Bulgart of Bay City, Michigan. Remarkably, most of the great Duck Island catch made its way to England. That the fish, packed in salted ice, were shipped across the ocean, shows the quality of the Georgian Bay catch.

The Duck Island fishing industry declined with the others and by 1914 only seven boats and 27 fishermen remained. The sawmill was closed in 1937 and moved to Cockburn Island. As late as the 1950s a few families still fished there and to this day an important lighthouse guides ships through the rough and rocky waters. Of the bustling 1890s fishing village there remains only the ruins of a wharf and the rotting lumber of the village buildings.

Georgian Bay's fishing industry became big business in the 1880s. Most fishermen were under licence to such large firms as Clark Brothers of Collingwood or C.W. Gauthier Company of Windsor. Then with the imposition of a 75-cent per hundredweight American tariff on Canadian fish in 1890, these two firms quickly found American partners and renamed themselves the Buffalo Fish Company and Detroit Fish Company.

The smaller firms were less lucky. Companies like Duffy, Noble and Purvis who commanded local fleets were still subject to the tariff. Never-

The road to the wharf leads past some of Burnt Island's buildings, only a few of which are still in use.

Many of Burnt Island's former dwellings now sit overgrown in a field.

theless, many like the Purvis family persevered and made fishing a way of life as well as an occupation.

By 1900, James, Edward and Alex Purvis operated fleets out of Providence Bay, Gore Bay and Meldrum Bay on Manitoulin Island. From their dry dock and freezer station in Gore Bay they hauled their catch of trout and whitefish across the North Channel to Blind River. From there C.P. trains carried the cargo to the Robert Beutel Fish Company in Bay City, Michigan.

The Purvis brothers reached **BURNT ISLAND** in the final years of the 19th century. This remote spot on the southwestern Manitoulin shoreline was misnamed Burnt "Island" because it was a peninsula that appeared to be an island to early observers. It became a busy fishing village and before long contained net sheds, an ice house, docks and a float factory. At its peak a dozen families occupied the wooden cabins along its solitary street.

At the turn of the century small boats still outnumbered the large tugs. In 1899 seven two-man skiffs or "mackinaws" bounced in the Burnt Island harbour. Powered by wind and muscle these small vessels were soon replaced by the Purvis' larger diesel tugs. These included the *Osprey, Flagship, Islet Prince* and the *Blue Fin,* now 50 years old and still active.

Purvis tugs have figured prominently in Georgian Bay lore. One day a frantic call came in from Great Duck Island that the lighthouse keeper had suffered a heart attack. The Purvis brothers powered up the *Blue Fin* and chugged towards that isolated rock. They carried the victim to hospital, but in this case the "attack" turned out to be pneumonia. In 1901 a Purvis tug rescued the crew from a burning lumber barge that had grounded on a shoal in the tricky waters near Little Current.

During the years of decline most of Burnt Island's families moved to larger towns and cities drawn by the lure of steady jobs. Today two or three homes remain occupied, but the rest stand vacant. Still dominating the centre of the village is the empty two-storey factory which once made fishing-net floats. Although the trout have gone, chubb and whitefish still find a market. As long as the Purvis' continue to fish as their family has done for a century, the village of Burnt Island will retain a spark of life.

Huddled off the mouth of the mighty French River, in the northeastern corner of Georgian Bay, are a clutch of 559 rocks, shoals and islets known as the **BUSTARD ISLANDS.** When summer fishing villages thrived, the Bustards had the second largest.

Commercial fishing started there around 1875, the year in which the Federal Department of Transport erected a small wooden lighthouse west of the main group on the Bustard Rocks. That was also the year James Pillgrem arrived from Meaford, built a cabin and began fishing. In the following years many other families followed, some from places like Meaford and Collingwood, others from Killarney on north Georgian Bay.

Despite the maze of islands and passages, the Bustards encircle a small but deep natural harbour. It was on the shores of this tiny harbour that most of the fishermen built their wooden shanties and tied their tugs. Its entrance is a long channel that is remarkably straight and narrow and earned the name "Gun Barrel".

Packing fish at a Georgian Bay summer fishing village. Steamers would arrive to carry the catch to railway terminals and from there it would be distributed to fish markets in Canada, America and as far away as England.

Fishing smacks jockey for space in the confines of Bustard Island's harbour. On the right sits a steam tugboat, one of the first of the craft which would replace sail.

James Cleland Hamilton visited the islands in 1893 and witnessed the unappetizing oil-making process. "On the Bustards the perfume carried about by an old man proclaimed him the keeper of the vats. Sitting in an oily scow he took the oars and passing out among the islands and into a little bay enclosed with large rocks we came to a shanty with an iron crane over the doorway and empty barrels about it." Hamilton entered the little laboratory with not a little reluctance. "Landing he ushered us into a crude laboratory. Noisesome messes stewed slowly in two iron vats, crude oil rising to the surface. He stirred up the simmering stuff unconscious of any unpleasantness as a painter mixing colours on his palette. Alas, our unaccustomed senses could not abide the terrible odours that arose. Waiting till his back was turned we escaped and were soon breathing purer air on a mossy rock top."

The Buffalo Fish Company, later the Dominion Fish Company, established its agent and shipping facilities on Ridout Island at the mouth of the Gun Barrel. For $70. per ton the agent purchased all the whitefish and trout the Bustards and other area fishermen could catch, and shipped them out, packed in ice, on the steamers *Manitou* and *Caribou*. After 1925 the steamer service ended and the fish were taken to Key Harbour where the CPR operated a busy coal dock. Here they were shipped via rail to southern Ontario and on to American markets.

During the 1930s the sea lamprey wiggled its way to northern Georgian Bay. Within a decade these blood suckers had nearly eliminated the lake trout and the Bustards' fishermen moved away. During the 1950s the cottage boom swept the Bay and urban dwellers from both the United States and Canada began to buy up the rugged islands.

Around the harbour a few old fishing cabins mingle with a small number of newer summer cottages. But the skiffs and tugs have long vanished. In their place are sleek yachts and cabin cruisers lying at anchor, sheltered from the sometimes wild winds of Georgian Bay, while their owners absorb the tranquillity of this distant island group.

Access to the Bustards is by boat only. Boat launch facilities exist at the village of Killarney, a one-time fishing village at the end of Highway 637, and from Highway 69 at either of two marinas at the head of Key Inlet. The watery passage then follows twisting back channels and rough shoal-ridden open waters. Charts and fair weather are necessities.

SPANISH MILLS

When J. B. McNeil looked through his grocery store window he saw a sea of floating logs. To his right and left 20 houses guarded a simple dirt trail. At the far end, looming over the rooftops, was the sawmill chimney belching white smoke into the blue northern sky.

The year was 1905 and McNeil had high hopes for the future of his village, Spanish Mills. Located on Aird Island four kilometers (2.5 miles) from the mouth of the Spanish River, it was the lumbering centre of Lake Huron's northern shore. Today the mills and the lumbering villages which sprung up around it are gone. Where a sea of logs and lumber tugs once floated in the bay there are now yachts and cruisers. While many of the early villages have become recreational homes, Spanish Mills was abandoned and deteriorated into a field of rubble.

It was 1860 when the lumbermen looked to the prize pine of the Spanish, French, Pickerel and Mississaugi Rivers' watersheds on Lake Huron's north shore. The swath of lumbering had laid bare Southern Ontario and Michigan and new stands of timber were needed. At first they simply boomed the logs across Lake Huron to mills in Michigan. A stiff American tarriff on imported rough lumber discouraged most lumbermen from building mills on the Ontario side. Finally Ontario's premier Oliver Mowat bowed to pressure from Ontario lumbermen and banned the export of uncut logs. American mill owners quickly moved to the north

Spanish Mills left few survivors of this its peak period in the 1920s. The school and a part of the mill are on the left, the store in the far distance.

Spanish Mills' lumbermen boomed and sorted logs in the mouth of the Spanish River for towing to their respective Lake Huron mills.

The large mills at Spanish Mills were for the first 30 years of this century the focus for a cluster of busy sawmill villages around the mouth of the Spanish River.

Only this cabin and shed survived Spanish Mills' fall. They stood until the mid-70s.

shore. One even "stole" his own mill and towed it across the international waters.

As a result, the north shore became crowded with roaring sawmills belching smoke into the northern skies. Around the mills were clustered boarding houses, schools, churches, stores and dozens of labourers' cabins. With the mines and the fishing stations, the north shore had become one of Canada's most industrialized shorelines.

By 1900 more than 20 different lumber companies were floating their winter log cut into the bay at Spanish Mills. It took 300 men of The Sable and Spanish River Boom and Lumber Company to sort and boom the logs to their respective mills.

During the short, warm north shore summers Spanish Mills throbbed with activity. On Saturdays the lumberjacks and millhands crowded into the wooden dance hall to tap their feet to the fiddle and guitar, but only a fortunate few found a blushing partner to lead into the square dance, for women were scarce in Spanish Mills.

Spanish Mills was a tough town that could look after itself. In addition to the dance hall and McNeil's store it contained a school and Presbyterian church. Most of the hardy residents lived in cramped conditions in a two-storey wooden boarding house. Their faces orange in the light of the coal oil lamps, they smoked, swapped ribald stories and talked of home. Supervisors and managers lived with their families year-round in the simple frame houses. The *Bon Ami* puffed between the island and the town of Spanish across the channel on the mainland.

Winter was a quiet time for Spanish Mills. The mills were shut and the lumberjacks had marched inland to cut red and white pine and stack it for the spring break-up.

As plentiful stands of wood got further away from town, Spanish Mills' existence became threatened. Finally, in 1927, the Spanish Mills Lumber

Company closed and moved to Skead to be closer to its limits. The mill was dismantled and moved. It was scant consolation to the dislocated loggers that theirs was the only north shore mill to be torn down. Every other mill was destroyed by fire and often not rebuilt, causing the mill towns to die.

The workers moved away, some taking their homes with them and skidding the buildings over the winter ice to Spanish where some still stand. Other buildings burned or decayed and collapsed. By 1970 only half a dozen empty shells remained. Today the view from McNeil's store site overlooks quiet waters and a weedy hillside. The single cabin and piles of lumber and cribbing are but pale reminders of the town's lost importance.

Although the negative plate was damaged years ago it still shows the interior of McNeil's store at Spanish Mills.

MOYLES MILLS

Bart Moyles looked again at his accounts ledger, but he knew there was no mistake. It was a losing proposition to operate a mill at Detour, Michigan when the supply of lumber lay across the bay on Huron's north shore. There was only one way out: steal his own mill. It meant removing it from under the noses of his creditors. Bart's brothers, George, John and James agreed it was the only way. The loose international laws of 1893 would protect them, if they could only get the equipment out of the U.S.

So began an adventure which warmed the heart of every con man who read about it.

Saying they wanted to improve the mill, the brothers and their most trusted workers started dismantling the machinery. Two lighters, or harbour boats, the *O.W. Chennie* and the *Annie Moiles* glided silently up to the sawmill wharf to load equipment. There remained only one obstacle: the two guards posted by the creditors to protect their holdings. One guard made a suprise discovery, a bottle of whiskey, while the other leapt on his horse and raced towards home when a Moyles man told him his young wife was sick. His wife was healthy, but his horse was not and collapsed some distance from the mill.

Within six hours the Moyles crew had loaded the machinery and frame onto the boats and by the time the sober guard got back they were 15 kilometres (10 miles) offshore. The local sheriff commandeered a fast boat and caught up to them. They were stuck in the ice, but it was Canadian ice. Three days later, free from the ice and with a sheriff waiting for them just over the border, they started re-assembling the mill at their new home, John Island.

Adjacent to Spanish Mills, John Island was in the heart of the timber country but they again failed to prosper and eventually sold to Guy Moulthorpe of Bay City, Michigan. Under the guidance of Moulthorpe and his partner Charles Moore the mill hummed profitably for 20 years. In 1908 the *Union Farmers Directory* described a community of 300 residents complete with a blacksmith, school, store, a Dr. Crok M.D. and a billiard parlour-cum-barber shop. More than 20 homes lined the rough shoreline road leading to the mill and by 1911 the number of houses had almost doubled to 36.

Then in 1918 the mill burned. As with other north shore mills the dwindling supplies did not warrant rebuilding. On the mainland the mill at Cutler continued to hum and the workers put their homes on floats and towed them across the channel to that site.

Today a YMCA camp occupies the one-time Moyles townsite. Beneath the waters of the little harbour lurk the sawdust and cribbings of Moyles' stolen mill.

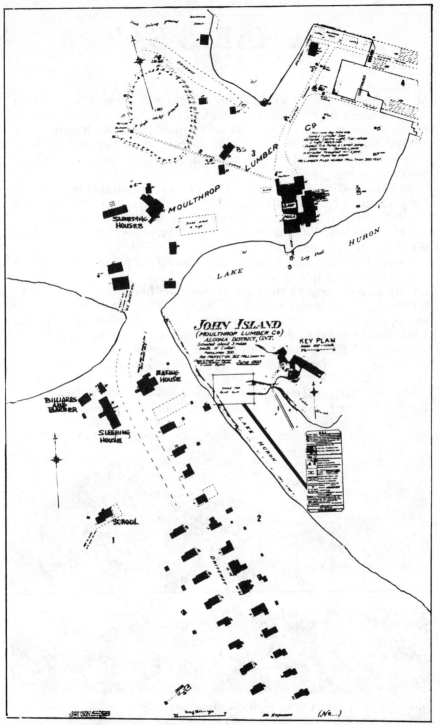

The size of the John Island village doubled in the years after Charles Goad prepared this insurance map in 1905.

MICHAELS BAY

Manitoulin Island is the world's largest freshwater island. Lying off Lake Huron's north shore, it lay in the path of the great 1860s and 70s lumbering boom. A Toronto entrepreneur named Lyons saw it coming and in 1868 built a sawmill on the Manitou River on the island's southeast shore. Rapids powered the mill while the sandy riverbank was ideal for workers' homes.

R. A. Lyons was touted as a scoundrel and perhaps that accounts for his political success as a member of the legislature. Nevertheless it was his mill, cutting timber allegedly stolen from beyond his legal limits that put Michaels Bay on the map. Although still on many maps, it has largely disappeared from the landscape.

"Stumptown", as Michaels Bay was first called, became Manitoulin's first permanent white settlement. Because it lay on the Huron shore it also became the port of entry for Manitoulin's homesteaders. In 1888 a townsite plan renamed the village Michaels Bay and surveyed out 18 blocks and 250 lots. Queen Street led to the dock 500 meters away while King Street wound through the bush to an upstart fishing station eight kilometers (5 miles) away named South Baymouth. However, the plan was largely ignored. Houses straddled lots and stood in the middle of roads.

Michaels Bay swelled to 20 houses, a store, blacksmith, school and two hotels. One, the Bayview House, became a popular destination for Amer-

Michaels Bay general store, with the proud proprietor standing at the front, was the focus for Manitoulin Island's first white settlement.

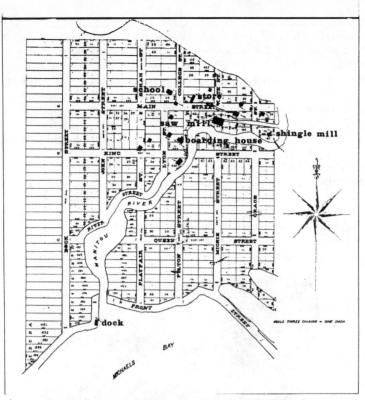

Plan of the village of Michaels Bay, Manitoulin Island.

ican tourists. While the mill and bushworkers pushed Michaels Bay's seasonal population to 400, the permanent population numbered 100. In 1906 the *Union Farmers Directory* reported that C. L. Wedgerfield ran the general store where Miss E. Wedgerfield made dresses. Robert Gault operated a post office, P. L. Clark a blacksmith shop and James Hilson made wagons. For a time the town was home to a colony of fishermen, however the protected harbour at South Baymouth eventually lured them from the more exposed shores at Michaels Bay.

The centre of the town's activity was Lyons' saw and shingle mill. Boards, lath, shingles, rails, posts and ties were piled onto trains and dragged over wooden rails to tugs and schooners waiting at the docks.

Although Lyons had paid only $2,000 for 60 square kilometers of timber he felt unencumbered by his boundaries and was accused of taking lumber from Crown Land. Furthermore, his personal bills put his Michaels Bay Trading Company seriously in debt. Then, in 1890 when his wooden mansion mysteriously burned, he sold out and fled to Toronto to lead the less hazardous life of a provincial member of the legislature.

By 1910 pioneer settlers had moved in and began burning the slash left by the lumberjacks. One such fire, unattended and whipped by sudden winds, raced towards Michaels Bay. Helpless to stop it, the towns-

69

people fled with what they could carry on their backs. When the flames finally died most of the cabins were smouldering ash. Disheartened, most turned their backs and moved inland. However, Mitchell's boarding house, the school and mill-manager's house survived until 1927 when the mill finally closed, its long-dwindling timber supply finally exhausted.

The intervening years have claimed almost all that was Michaels Bay. Only the school stood until recently. Now depressions, the mill foundations and the cribbing from the King St. bridge are all that remain. Even survey posts placed by nearby residents to mark the former building sites have disappeared.

Meanwhile the upstart fishing village of South Baymouth, once so dependent on Michaels Bay, has become the hub of southeastern Manitoulin. In the summer, the government ferry, M. S. Chi-Cheemaun, disgorges 600 passengers and 115 cars and trucks four times a day. While South Baymouth has become Manitoulin's port of entry, its predecessor, Michaels Bay, lies forgotten by all but a few older residents.

The cribbings of the King St. bridge which led to a once busy pioneer farming settlement east of Michaels Bay.

FRENCH RIVER

"Next day we visited French River, a great lumber centre with two mills, immense piles of pine boards and long elevated tramways for the removing and hauling of the timber," wrote James Cleland Hamilton in his 1893 travel book, *The Georgian Bay*. He travelled the wild northeastern coastline by steamer and of the many lumber towns he visited, French River stuck in his mind as the largest.

The town began modestly. Located in the Main Channel of the French River it originated with Sam Wabb's trading post and by 1883 had become Wabb Town, a small log booming and shipping village. Here the Ontario government surveyed a town plot which it called Copananing. The Walkerton Lumber Company cut its logs up the French River, boomed them to the mouth of the river and towed them to mills in Michigan. French River had no mill then and the eight small wooden cabins were occupied only during the navigable months.

In 1883 Herman Cook formed the Ontario Lumber Company and moved into the French River area in a major way. He bought the existing timber licences, surveyed his own townsite adjacent to Copananing and built the great mills. The village boomed and spilled over onto the government plan. Houses were built anywhere the soil could support them.

French River's doctor prepares medicine for a couple of apprehensive young patients. Village doctors came complete with their own small pharmacy where they mixed powders and elixirs for their patients. Other potions, often of dubious merit, were available at the general store.

Rugged rocky terrain at French River defied efforts to lay out streets and build village homes.

By 1900 the town could boast two dozen houses, a boarding house, two general stores (one operated by H. Benoit, the other by original settler Sam Wabb), W.J. Fraser's barber shop and three hotels: the Queens, the Copananing and Kelly's. Villagers worshipped in the Catholic or Presbyterian churches which stood side by side in the Copananing townsite and sent their children to the public or separate schools. The town was headquarters for the French River Boom and Rafting Company, the French River Tug Company and the Irwin and Co. log jobbers, who did custom lumbering jobs. Although local sources estimate the population at more than 1,000, the 1906 *Union Farmers Directory* reported a population of 200 and in 1908, 350.

The 50-foot mill stack dominated the town. Wooden tramways carried waste to the burners while on the shoreline great piles of lumber awaited shipment and often prevented steamers from making their scheduled stops, as Hamilton discovered. The shops and hotel were clustered around the wharf while the frame cabins nestled in wavering rows between the rock ridges. So barren was the townsite that sawdust was dumped in the rocky gullies to make rudimentary roads.

By the turn of the century wealthy city dwellers had discovered the beauty of Georgian Bay and crowded aboard the steamers. One hotel proprietor, S. Phillips, advertised that "Tourists will find that the Queens Hotel is a first class house. Good fishing and shooting in close proximity. The wines, liquors and cigars are the best." Every Tuesday and Friday at 6 p.m. the steamer *Norbelle* departed Collingwood carrying tourists to French River as well as to Parry Sound, Bying Inlet and Killarney.

By 1910 French River was in decline. The best timber in the area had been recklessly razed and lumbermen had to venture far afield to find fresh stands. As well, the CPR had completed its line through the hinterland. A railside location provided the lumber companies with a means of shipment year round. The seasonal waterways did not. Finally, in 1912, the Ontario Lumber Company moved its mills to Pine Lake and most of the townspeople dispersed.

Dean Udy managed to keep the store open with the lodge and cottage trade until 1922, then he too moved. Buildings were disassembled; some collapsed where they stood. Today, rotting lumber, half-buried by bush, litters the rocky outcrops and in the water lurk cribbing and rusting boilers. The only visible survivors are the stone base of the lumber company chimney and the little white lighthouse. These meagre remains are accessible only by boat. The nearest launching facilities are at Key River 15 kilometers (9 miles) east and at Killarney, the same distance west. A part of each route crosses open water that can become treacherous at times, but the quiet French River mouth with its uncounted pink granite islands is one of cottage country's few undeveloped wilderness shorelines.

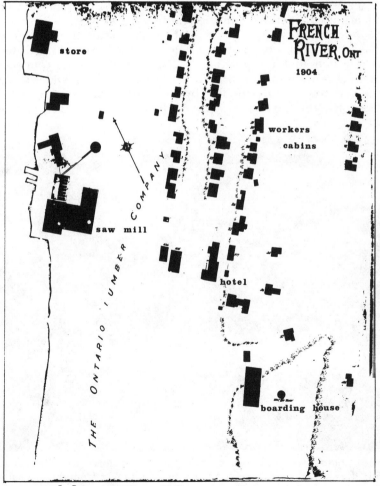

Town plan of French River, 1904.

73

SPRAGGE

Boaters who venture too close to Narrow Point risk running into the sunken hull of the 252-foot *Winona,* a remnant of one frantic night at the north shore lumbering town of Spragge.

The veteran bay steamer caught fire at the Spragge dock. As the flames licked towards the lumber piles on shore, the crew and lumber workers frantically worked to get a line aboard the burning ship and tow it across the channel. When they reached Narrow Point, it flared and sank.

In 1900 north shore lumbering was at its peak. In or near the mouth of the Spanish River there were more than a dozen mills. One of the largest and most widely known was Spragge. In 1873 Hiram and George Cook acquired extensive lumber rights along the Serpent River and in 1883 they built Spragge's first mill at the river mouth. After just 15 years, Spragge could boast two hotels, a railway station, general store, doctor, barber, school and a population of 250. A daily steamer connected it with neighbouring mill towns. Workers' cabins stood shoulder to shoulder in neat rows on the sand flats by the wharves while the larger homes and a hotel crowned a craggy promontory behind. Further west along

These two photos (see bottom of page 75) show a panorama of Spragge's harbour, including the six berths once used by tugs to load lumber from the large mill.

74

the shore were the school, hospital and cemetery. At the shore a half-dozen berths accommodated such tugs as the *N. Dyment*, the *John R. Stover* and the *Waubaushene*.

The docks were the scene of various maritime accidents, including the burning of the *Winona*. Another happened when the *Seymour*, which chugged between Spragge and Spanish River, crashed into the *Alert* tied at the dock. Two men were pitched to their doom in the frigid waters.

In 1907 the Waldie brothers bought out the Cooks and promptly closed the mill, preferring to boom the logs across Georgian Bay to their larger mills at Victoria Harbour. Spragge's depression, however, lasted just six years. In 1903 James S. McFadden had appeared on the scene. Lured from Aylmer, Quebec, by the north shore's promising pine stands, McFadden formed a partnership with John Malloy and quickly acquired north shore limits and many of its mills. In 1913 he moved his head-quarters to Spragge. For 20 years the north shore buzzed to the sounds of McFadden's mills in Nesterville, Blind River, and in the town of Spragge. By 1931, however, his timber limits were nearly depleted. Fires at Nesterville and two tragic fires within three years at the Spragge mill, forced him to concentrate his milling in Blind River and to close his other mills. Gradually, as the town's residents moved away, Spragge dis-appeared. Buildings which weren't moved were burned where they stood.

Then in 1948 a glimmer of new life appeared. Prospector Karl Gun-termann discovered radioactive rocks. In 1953 J. H. Hirschborn founded

See photo at bottom of page 74.

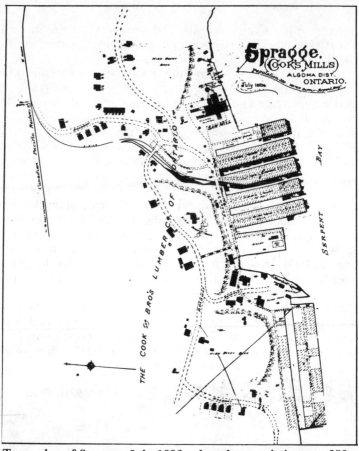

Town plan of Spragge, July 1896, when the population was 350.

Until the 1920s Spragge was an important mill town. A weedy field is now all that is left of these workers' cabins.

the Pronto Uranium Mine and on October 15, 1955 began production near the old Spragge mill. By 1960 the Pronto had produced 3.6-million tons, not of uranium, but copper. Falling copper prices in 1961 forced Hirschborn to close the mine, but the Pronto Mill continued to process ore from the nearby Pater mine. Ten years later the Pronto had produced a further 78-million pounds of copper along with small amounts of gold and silver. Then it too fell silent.

Today there is a third Spragge. A string of stores and houses along busy Highway 17, one mile from the harbour, has grown out of highway tourism and pulp mill jobs in Espanola 50 kilometers (30 miles) east.

Meanwhile the original Spragge of the Waldies and the Cooks and of McFadden lies in a quiet field beside Serpent Harbour. The six tug berths, now overgrown with lilies and cattails, are its most visible remnant. The great stone walls of the mill hide behind lilacs and sumachs while across the sand and on the hill lie the foundations of the village homes. Today's tranquillity is broken only by a few campers who seek the waterside stillness of the north shore, a contrast to the noisy days when lumber was king of Spragge.

VICTORIA MINES

"How embarassing," thought Judge McNaughton, "for a provincial court judge to be lost." The forests north of Sudbury in 1882 had no roads and few paths. To wander from the trail even a few yards invited disaster, whether one was experienced or not in the bush. As he sat on a rock to ponder his next move, McNaughton, an amateur geologist, sighted a rock bearing copper and momentarily forgot his predicament.

Two years later, long after McNaughton had found his way home, a CPR construction crew blasted open the same rock outcrop. The rock fragments flashed with nickel and McNaughton's copper was soon forgotten. As a branch of the CPR inched westward from Sudbury each dynamite charge seemed to uncover new nickel riches. Headframes shot skyward at Creighton, Lively, Frood and, 40 kilometers (24 miles) west of Sudbury at Victoria Mines.

Prospector Henry Roger first discovered the nickel at the Victoria Mines' site in 1886. Once rail access was established, an Austrian geologist named Ludwig Mond, anxious to test a new extracting process, bought the claim and Victoria Mines quickly acquired a mill and townsite.

Victoria Mines grew into a bustling community. In 1906 the *Union Farmers Directory* listed five general stores, a restaurant, barber and doctor and a population of 1,000. In 1910 the *Bradstreet Directory* also listed a pool hall, blacksmith, baker, butcher, men's clothing store and railway

A road sign announces a mine which isn't there.

None of these buildings on Victoria Mine's main street survived the demise of the mine.

Ludwig Mond introduced a new nickel smelting process to North America at the Victoria Mine smelters.

station. The town plot with 200 lots and a dozen streets hugged the railway line while a short distance away another town named Ranger was surveyed, but remained only a paper dream.

Victoria Mines was plagued with misfortune. In 1907, the tramway burned. The following year, 1908, saw an act of forgotten heroism in which nothing but the names and actions of two men remains. One day a tapper named Bezanthe alerted the mine foreman Guran that the settling furnace was reaching dangerously high temperatures. With little thought for their own safety, they raced about the noisy mine warning the 100 other miners to flee for their lives. For some unexplained reason, possibly to try and get the temperature down, they remained in the mill. During the fiery explosion that followed, they met their end.

Victoria's deposit was hard to mine: it went straight down. While boasting Ontario's deepest shaft (by 1918 it had been sunk nearly a kilometer) the miners had little choice but to keep digging and the costs finally grew too high. By 1920 as the deposit began to thin out the owners laid off most of the 275-man work force. In 1923 they shut the mine completely and moved the equipment and men several kilometers east to the Frood Extension Mine.

Victoria Mines quickly shrivelled. Houses were moved or burnt and by 1930 the only business left was Oliver Brassard's store. Today ten kilometers (six miles) from Whitefish and the Trans Canada Highway several cindered streets follow their grid pattern through a weedy meadow. Only two of the old miners' cabins survive as a reminder of the days when Victoria Mines was a leader in the Sudbury field.

At Victoria Mines only two miners' cabins have survived from a town that once had 1,000 residents. As is obvious from the laundry on the line, they are still in use.

OPHIR

The first glittering metal brought out of Northern Ontario was copper. A trade item long used by the Ojibway, it drew mining companies to the shores of Huron and Superior long before the pioneer settlers. The first operations on Huron's north shore occurred east of present day Sault Ste. Marie at a place called Bruce Mines. Between the 1840s and 80s the noisy mills brought the birth of a sizeable community, and later, as the feverish mining activities slowed, settlers.

On a chill November morning William Moore studied the walls of a giant cliff. Moore was one of the farmers who started moving into the sheltered, fertile vales tucked between Algoma's spectacular mountain. ridges in 1889. Just 25 kilometers (15 miles) north of the copper mining town of Bruce Mills, the settler found what trained prospectors, with their eyes to the ground, had missed. High above his head, amongst the grey granite and white quartz, shone the unmistakable glint of gold.

Moore quickly climbed the cliff and chipped off a piece of the shiny rock. It was fool's gold, he thought to himself, and he was the fool car-

The Rock Lake mine was one of the two gold mines in the Ophir gold field. This spectacular building was the mill, with the powerhouse stack on left.

Ophir village has survived in remarkably good condition and is an untrammelled example of a mining village at the turn of the century. Its brief history, from 1892 to 1912, and its isolation mean few changes have taken place in the village.

rying it into town for an assay. But his find ignited a fierce quarrel over ownership until 1892 when an American group, the Ophir Gold Mining Company of Duluth, Minnesota, settled the confusion by buying the land.

In short order Ophir sank two shafts, built a 20-stamp mill and constructed a small village for its 30 employees. In the little settlement stood the manager's house, a cook house and dining room, bunkhouses, two offices, a store, blacksmith and various storehouses associated with the mine.

The mill clattered away noisily for two years. Then late in the winter of 1894, as the frost began to work its way out of the ground, a fold— or vein—of rock in the ceiling of the shaft tumbled loose. Rocks and dirt rumbled into the hole. Beneath the rubble three bodies lay crushed.

The Ontario Bureau of Mines ordered an immediate halt to the operation until it could complete an investigation. On March 9 an angry inspector, T. W. Gibson reported the incident: "Before any further work is done, I direct that substantial supports be placed in the mine... have the surface openings properly fenced. Also put side railings on the tramway leading from the mine to the mill." By July 17, Francis Taylor, the mine manager, had completed Gibson's orders but the mine did not reopen. Depressed gold prices delayed production and when they had not improved a year later, the mine closed.

In 1902 the Bruce Mines and Algoma Railway built a spur line from Bruce Mines to the nearby Rock Lake mine and made it possible for the Havilah Gold Mining Company to reopen the Ophir mill in 1909. Once more the little valley bristled with life. In addition to the two gold mines were James Stevenson's sawmill, a general store and a post office. The *Union Farmers Directory* listed the area's population at 300.

By 1912 the price of gold no longer mattered for the veins were dry.

In 1916 Ontario Bureau of Mines inspectors found the mill collapsing and the town empty and overgrown. Although no trace remains of the mill or tramway today, the other buildings, offices, bunkhouses and homes stand in a tight cluster, gazing windowless over the green pastures of the Ophir valley, beneath the golden cliff which brought them to life.

The site lies 25 kilometers (15 miles) north of Bruce Mines, 2.5 kilometers (1.5 miles) northwest of the junction of secondary highways 561 and 638. The double row of empty, solid buildings may be small, but their mountain and pasture setting evoke a ghost town image reminiscent of the American southwest gold rush.

Ophir's mine office and dwellings now stare quietly over the lush pastoral valley northeast of Sault Ste. Marie.

ARDBEG

By 1900 the tall pines which had shaded Georgian Bay's watershed were gone. The railways, however, opened forests that were once remote and gave birth to a string of new mill towns throughout the district of Parry Sound. One of the busiest was Ardbeg.

Its lifeblood was its sawmills—Ardbeg rose and, ultimately, fell with them. Hayward and Son, the town's first sawmillers, lasted only a few years. Then in 1911 L. Robertson opened a larger mill with a daily capacity of 25,000 board feet and the town began to boom. By the time the large lumber firm of Tudhope and Ludgate erected its mill in 1922 the town was in its prime.

Ardbeg grew in the form of a "T". At the base was the railway station, at the top the store. Balancing the limbs stood the virtue and vice of all small towns: the church at one end and the pool room at the other. Along the streets were more than two dozen frame houses. Earl Bottrell took time off cutting hair in his barber shop to serve up ice cream to the schoolchildren. Two hotels, Frank Dutcher's and the Evans', boarded lumbermen during the busy season and the occasional tourist during the summer. Walter Leitch operated the first store and post office, passing it on to MacMillan, then Angus Robertson took over. The last proprieter was Fleming. After their shifts in the noisy mill or on the trains, the men found their way to the poolroom, which was nothing more than a pool table shoved into a seedy back room. Saturday nights often resounded to the music from Laflemme's dance hall. During the peak periods when

An aerial view of Ardbeg taken from the fire tower shortly after its completion in the 1930s. The hotel and one of the stores are in the lower left.

Ardbeg was originally called Deer Lake by the railway during the days when self-propelled passenger coaches provided service along the line.

lumberjacks crowded in from the forests, Ardbeg's two streets bustled with more than 1,000 people.

As with most lumber towns, fire was an ever-present threat. In 1919 a forest fire swept the town destroying many of its wooden structures, but the tenacious residents rebuilt and carried on as before. Soon afterwards fire destroyed a wooden trestle on the railway. Until it could be fixed, passengers had to disembark from one train, cross a sometimes frigid creek on foot and scramble up the opposite bank to board a second train waiting to carry them on their voyage. Eventually, to reduce the threat of unexpected fire, the Ontario Department of Lands and Forests constructed a wooden fire tower.

An advertisement in the *Canadian Lumberman and Woodworker* magazine was the first indication to the outside world that Ardbeg was in trouble. It offered for sale a steam engine, balance wheel, steam feeder carriage and "one 50-foot smokestack". The seller was L. Robertson of Ardbeg. The year was 1928.

For 10 years Robertson's mill stood lifeless and unwanted, as if to mock Ardbeg's better days. Finally in 1938 a man by the name of Zagerman from Ottawa bought the weathered old structure... for scrap. By 1941 the population had slipped to 146. During the 40s Maynard and Bennett operated small mills, but between them employed only 17 men.

Ardbeg's slide continued into the 50s and 60s. By 1976 its population had tumbled to 38 and most of its prominent buildings had gone. In 1963 Butcher's Hotel burned to the ground; in 1969 the CNR dismantled its station. In 1971 the Department of Lands and Forests replaced the fire tower with air surveillance and in 1976 dismantled its remaining buildings. In the same year Walter Leitch's old store came down.

Ardbeg is diminished but not dead. A new store with restaurant caters to summer cottagers from the many nearby lakes and to the few remaining permanent residents. Of the town's early key buildings only the Evans Hotel, the one-time poolroom, the school and a few dwellings remain.

Trains no longer stop in Ardbeg, however, road improvements have made the old village easily accessible by car. It lies 45 kilometers (27 miles) north of Highway 124 from a junction 30 kilometers (18 miles) east of the town of Parry Sound. These road improvements have arrested the area's decline and it is fast becoming a popular cottage area. The old town however, still offers a fascinating glance back to another era.

Leitch's general store at Ardbeg sat vacant until the 1970s when this photo was taken. Just visible under the veranda roof are the building's original stained glass windows.

LOST CHANNEL PAKESLEY

Lost Channel and Pakesley, twin ghost towns with many empty buildings and shells of houses still in place, date back to one of the earliest lumbering ventures in northern Parry Sound.

From deep in Parry Sound's prime timber country, the Pickerel River plunges through granite gorges to Georgian Bay and once provided an important logging link between the inland pine stands and the mills on the Bay. The area's first timber licence was granted in the 1890s to Victoria Harbour Lumber Company. It boomed its logs across Kawigamog Lake, sent them hurtling down the Pickerel and towed them south over Georgian Bay to its mills. It was on one of these drives that company foreman "Black Jack" Kennedy boomed the logs into what he thought was the lake's outlet to the river. Despite its wide appearance, the "channel" ended abruptly at a swampy bay. Nonplussed, Kennedy, whose name Black Jack was a common moniker for those of Irish descent, boomed the logs back out the dead-end channel and on towards the river. He named the bay "Lost Channel". For several years its sole occupant was the small dock and warehouse of Captain Edgar Walton, captain of the steamboat *Douglas*.

Loading timber the old way on the Key Valley Railway at Lost Channel.

Engineers in training? These ladies posed on one of the steam engines of the Key Valley Railway at Pakesley.

Then, in 1914, the Lauder Spears and Howland Company bought the Victoria limits and erected a mill beside Kennedy's Lost Channel. At first it teamed the logs over a rugged bush trail to a lumber siding at Mowat 20 kilometers (12 miles) south of Lost Channel, but the road was rugged and often impassable. Mired wheels and broken axles forced the company to replace the troublesome route with a new railway which led directly west for 16 kilometers (10 miles) to the CPR siding at Pakesley. Before the Lauder Company could finish it, the Schroeder Mills and Timber Company bought up the financially troubled Lauder in 1917 and drove the last spike on the Key Valley Railway (KVR).

On a peninsula beside the Lost Channel, Schroeder replaced Lauder's bunkhouses with an entirely new townsite. After building a new bunkhouse and cookery, he added a general store, hospital and free school and, around the shore of the peninsula, he placed a dozen cabins for millworkers and their families.

The mill became the area's largest operation. Three storeys in height, it could slash through a million board feet of lumber every week.

Mill manager James Ludgate was a man ahead of his time. In a day when wanton razing of the forest was standard procedure, Ludgate offered this conservation warning: "Why all this big hurry to cut up our forests and lose money? We should conserve instead, but we imagine we must keep moving full blast or we will die of ennui." In Ontario this message bears constant repeating.

A second village developed at the railway junction. Here, where the Key Valley Railway met the busy CPR, Schroeder's great lumber piles awaited shipment to Detroit, Chicago or New York. Up until then Pakesley had been a sleepy sectional village with its bunkhouses, offices, station, water tower and coal dock. But when the KVR entered town, Pakesley boomed. Almost overnight it added a post office, hotel and a restaurant called "Middy's". In 1924 the CPR built a new station with a concrete foundation and seven rooms to accommodate the agent and his family. The Department of Lands and Forests added a fire tower and ranger's quarters. During its heyday Pakesley's 30 buildings lined dirt roads on both sides of the track.

The KVR trains ran twice daily between the villages with passengers, freight and six carloads of logs, linking the fortunes of Pakesley inseparably with those of Lost Channel.

In August of 1927, perhaps realizing his limits were nearing exhaustion, Schroeder sold the mill to James Playfair of Midland who renamed it the Pakesley Lumber Company. Within three years Playfair's luck turned bad. On November 1, 1930 a mechanic repairing two locomotives in the machine shop let a careless spark fly. Within minutes the shop was a raging inferno and the flames spread quickly to the mill. The ice was thick on the lake and the workers could not chop fast enough to fill water buckets to try and contain the blaze. The mill crashed down in a shower of sparks.

Undaunted, Playfair, knowing that the timber cutting season was fast approaching, set crews to rebuild the mill. Until he could install new machinery he cut his timber in a nearby abandoned mill. Within weeks the Lost Channel mill was roaring again.

A survivor of Lost Channel's milling days is slowly being reclaimed by a young forest.

89

Its echoes were to be short-lived. By then most of Parry Sound's valuable timber was gone and lumbering had moved north. In 1933 Playfair closed his mill and sold it for scrap. The employees took a last look at their homes in Lost Channel, turned their backs and left.

Pakesley's death was slower. Even after the sidings were lifted in 1935 the railwaymen stayed. Following the Second World War the railway centralized and Lands and Forests replaced the fire tower with air surveillance. The post office and store survived until 1956, the station until 1971. Many of Pakesley's buildings, although empty, still stand in good repair. Overgrown and windowless they present a forlorn and ghostly spectre.

Highway 522 passes through Pakesley six kilometers (3.5 miles) east of the Trans Canada Highway (69). This dusty road then follows part of the KVR roadbed to the remains of Lost Channel.

Time has claimed much of the old town. One by one, under the weight of snow and weakened by rot, the houses on the wooded peninsula sag a little more each year. Cribbing from the steamer dock survives in the shallow inlet, while the Key Valley railbed itself is now a cottage road. Schroeder's boarding house, still standing and with a fresh coat of white paint, thrives as an attractive summer lodge.

A row of abandoned houses at Pakesley.

BRENT

On a remote lake in northeastern Algonquin Park stand the wooden cabins and weathered store that were once Brent. In 1914 the Canadian Northern Railway plunged through Algonquin Park between Pembroke and North Bay and spawned a string of villages with names like Daventry, Achray, Lake Traverse and Government Park which boomed briefly around mills or stations and then faded. When the line opened in 1914 it needed a divisional point. The sandy northern shoreline of Cedar Lake seemed ideal. It was halfway between North Bay and Pembroke and the flat backshore could support a substantial townsite. Soon Brent bustled with 30 houses, a store, restaurant, bunkhouse and maintenance sheds. For a schoolhouse the children had to make do with a converted railway car.

In 1921 the Brent Lumber Company started up a large sawmill on a point of land at the west end of the village. A Hawkesbury lumber company had previously occupied the site and prior to the railway had constructed a 50-kilometer (30-mile) tote road to haul logs to the Ottawa River. The rest house at the halfway point still stands.

Although the mill lasted only ten years, Brent was foremost a railway town and despite the disappearance of the Brent Lumber Company the village continued to grow. Gery McGaughy took over the general store, George Mathiew the restaurant and in 1941 the permanent population topped 150. Finally the Nipissing Board of Education replaced the old

A part of the village of Brent with the old general store on the right. The sign on the door says "open".

91

A number of old railway houses at Brent are now summer cottages.

Another CNR milltown in Algonquin Park was Daventry west of Brent. At various times it had two mills and this school house where up to 16 pupils sat through eight grades in the same room.

railway car with a permanent school house for the 40 pupils. The school filled many functions. On Saturday nights it would echo to the strains of the fiddle and the stomping of feet and on Sunday mornings weary revellers trudged back to it for a sermon from an itinerant pastor. Perhaps the occasional sermon cautioned against the excesses of the previous night's carousing.

During the 1960s the CNR discontinued passenger service. Brent's villagers suddenly depended once more upon the ancient tote road for access, but the Department of Lands and Forests refused to plough the road in winter. For much of the year villagers were cut off from the outside. In 1978, as disgruntled residents fled, the school and post office were closed (although, following a determined protest by Brent's townsfolk and then federal member of parliament Leonard Hopkins, the post office re-opened briefly). The die was cast. When the way freight no longer appeared with its regular supply of food, Gery McGaughy had to close his store. Out of 160 residents only three remained behind.

McGaughy was one of the last to leave. "Over the years we knew what was coming," he said in the *North Bay Nugget* newspaper, "but we figured this was a damn good place to get ready to die in." Gery McGaughy almost got his wish. In 1980 he died, not in Brent, but in a railway car en route to a North Bay Hospital.

Most of Brent still stands. A row of cabins lines the track as it has for 60 years. The old wooden store is now owned by the Ministry of Natural Resources and is leased to a summer outfitter who supplies canoeists and campers. The school, restaurant and old bunkhouse still see occasional use as summer cottages. In the centre of the village, in stark contrast to the old buildings, stands the new CNR bunkhouse, an aluminum motel-like building, for although the village has been vacated, the site remains CN's divisional point. If the Ministry of Natural Resources had its way, Brent, like the other Algonquin Park villages, would be destroyed, but most of the buildings lie in the CN right-of-way and out of the reach of the Ministry's bulldozers. The ghostly remains of Brent will likely be around for some time to come.

The old tote road remains Brent's only access. This twisting 50-kilometer (30-mile) dirt route leaves Highway 17 at Deux Rivieres and rewards the visitor with a well preserved early railway division town.

KIOSK/FOSMILL

The largest town ever to exist within the boundaries of Algonquin Park is not dead, but it is dying. By refusing to sell the townspeople their leased lots, the Ontario government is forcing them out. The bulldozers sit poised nearby.

In 1910 S. J. Staniforth and William Foster could not have known their paths would cross. Staniforth had completed his fourth year as an accountant with the giant Fassett Lumber Company in Fassett, Quebec, while William Foster operated a small sawmill near the northern boundary of Algonquin Park.

By 1924 Staniforth had become the president of Fassett. With Quebec's pine stripped away, Staniforth sent John McGibbon to appraise the timber across the border in Ontario. Because Foster's mill had remained modest, his limits inside Algonquin were well stocked. For Staniforth it was an opportunity to rejuvenate his company's sagging empire. For Foster it was a chance to retire wealthy.

At the Fosmill siding Staniforth built a town. Along the track he built 35 homes, some one-and-one-half storeys high and large enough to accommodate three families. Soon afterwards he built a wooden schoolhouse where 53 pupils fidgeted through the eight primary grades.

Fosmill in many respects suffered the cultural division found in many lumber communities in Ontario and Quebec. While mill and bush workers were French, staff supervisors and executives were English. The separation was physical as well as cultural. The French were Catholic, the English were Protestant and each worshipped independently. Separate living quarters kept the English supervisor from the French worker. The

A view of Kiosk, the town that Staniforth built. The earlier Booth bunkhouse is the white building in the centre.

Staniforth's great mill at Kiosk burned in 1975 a few years after this photo was taken, giving the Ontario government the excuse to begin destroying the village.

company boarding house was home to the French; Mrs. McFail's private hostel hosted office staff and visitors.

Staniforth's mills soon became the largest in northeastern Ontario. A 650-horsepower engine drove the great saws year round with enough excess energy to provide electricity for the entire village. Six hundred men worked in the mill or in one of the camps on Little Moose, Big Moose, Tea or Manitou Lakes. Seventy teams of horses drew the logs to a 20-kilometer (12-mile) narrow gauge railway along which the small puffing steam engines hauled them to the mill.

Two disastrous fires in three years wrote the end of the town's story. In 1932 smoke was spotted in the lumber yard. As workers ran with fire hoses, the dry piles exploded into flames. Worker and supervisor toiled together, keeping the bucking hoses trained on the fire and bringing in pumps and water to prevent the conflagration from consuming the mill. In 1932 they succeeded, but in 1934 they were not so lucky. One of Ontario's greatest mills burned to the ground that year.

Upon learning that the large limits of the J. R. Booth company only 18 kilometers (10 miles) to the east were available, Staniforth obtained permission from the province to erect a mill and town within the limits of Algonquin Park. A year later he moved to this new site, Kiosk, and Fosmill died. By 1940 the 35 houses in Fosmill had dwindled to 16 and by 1955 to six. Today, not one building stands and the road has become impassable to everything but all-terrain vehicles.

Kiosk straddled the main line of the CNR and before Staniforth came contained only a handful of CNR section buildings and a small Booth lumber camp with a store, bunkhouse and cookery. These, however,

No sooner does a Kiosk resident move away than the government bulldozer moves in and reduces the house to rubble.

would soon be swallowed up by Algonquin Park's largest ever town. On the shore of the lake beside the old Booth camp Staniforth built his mill. For the first few years his operations remained uncharacteristically modest, the population of 75 housed in the Booth bunkhouse or one of a handful of cabins along the track. In 1938 he acquired a post office and named it Kiosk, the shortened name of Lake Kioshkakwi, on whose north shore the town sits.

Staniforth carefully planned his new empire. In 1943, on the east side of the river overlooking his mill, he built the first of two townsites. On the west bank of the river he added a second townsite. As the population swelled to 250 the town acquired a Roman Catholic church, a new four-room school and piped water. Electricity came from a small power plant on the river.

After work and on weekends, the townsfolk would gather at the baseball diamond, skating rink or recreation hall in the former school. Although never an incorporated municipality, Kiosk was governed by a small elected council who supervised electricity, water supply and snow ploughing.

Kiosk kept growing and by 1961 its 350 residents lived in 75 houses. Despite the arrival of a paved highway the town never realized the full range of stores and services that a place of its size would normally expect. Typical of a company town, no store was allowed to compete with the single company store. And liquor, at least technically, was prohibited.

In 1969 Staniforth's lease expired and trouble began. Having determined that a residential community is not a use appropriate for a provincial park, the Ontario Department of Lands and Forests refused to renew the mill lease for more than one year at a time. Four years later when the huge mill burned to the ground, the government denied him permission to rebuild. The timber limits were still good so Staniforth rebuilt a few miles outside the park boundary and residents easily commuted the short distance. Although they owned their Kiosk homes they did not own the land and the Department, now known as the Ministry of Natural Resources, wanted it back. Their park "master plan" designated the area as "wilderness" and homes did not belong.

Kiosk refused to fall without a fight. Recruiting federal and provincial politicians, residents pleaded for their homes and offered to exchange a private wilderness area adjacent to the Park for their town. The Ministry remained unmoved.

The townsfolk did, however, win a small victory: those who wish may now remain until 1996. Others who wish to leave receive enough compensation for their homes to relocate comfortably elsewhere, but scarcely are they out the door when the Ministry bulldozer, lurking nearby, moves in to plough their home into history.

Kiosk, or what remains of it, lies at the end of Highway 630 about 80 kilometers (48 miles) southeast of North Bay. About half the houses, along with the church and school, still stand as does the town's oldest building, Booth's boarding house.

Kiosk lives on borrowed time, a ghost town in the making. It is another case where the Ontario government has turned its back on its own heritage. In the name of "wilderness" it obliterates all historical buildings and towns within the Park. Kiosk was just one that got in the Ministry's way.

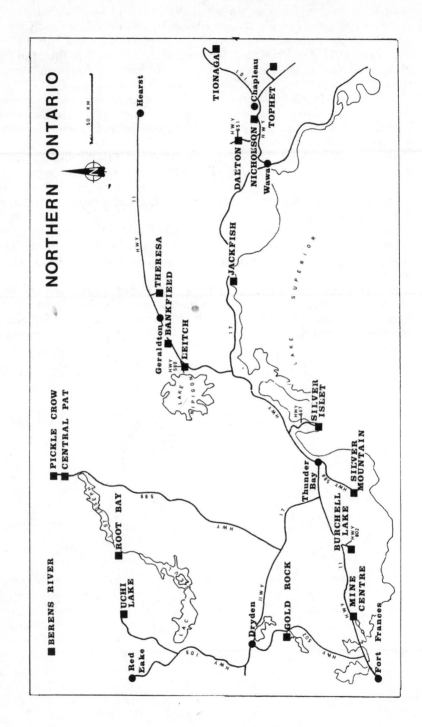

NORTHERN ONTARIO

SECTION THREE
NORTHERN ONTARIO

Beyond Superior's spectacular shores, beyond the lapping waters of Lake Huron, a multitude of lakes feed rivers that flow through the birch and spruce wilderness toward the Arctic and Hudson Bay. This is northern Ontario, a land of long and cold winters, of vast spaces filled with rock, sand and muskeg. This forbidding and challenging land is also rich in natural resources, a wealth that attracted enterprising people, spawned its boom towns and, ultimately, its ghost towns.

All that had to wait for the railways. Prior to the 1880s the northland was dotted with Indian villages and fur posts. The only towns were a few small fishing villages and short-lived mining camps that ringed Lake Superior. The legendary Silver Islet was the sole exception.

During the 1880s, the CPR snaked its way northwest from Sudbury into the pine forests. In its wake came a string of sawmills and tie mills and the little company towns that sprang up around them.

The line then swung westward along the mountainous shores of Lake Superior. Sleepy fishing villages were suddenly transformed into busy shipping towns. At the Lakehead, the railway edged inland once more to cut through the spruce and tamarack forests towards the vast prairies.

Other lines followed. Two development railways, the Temiskaming and Northern Ontario (now The Ontario Northland) and the Algoma Central wound northward from North Bay and Sault Ste. Marie respectively in the first decade of this century. By 1915 two more transcontinental links were open: the Canadian Northern which largely paralleled the CPR and the National Transcontinental which traversed the far north. All had the same effect: as the only form of transportation, they became the focus for village development. Every few kilometers were the section villages and every 200 kilometers (125 miles) the important divisional towns. The mill towns developed close to the railways or water-power sites.

Nearly all were company towns. Typically each had its store, boarding house, worker's cabins and executive homes. Larger towns could boast churches, schools, recreational halls and sometimes movie theatres. Beginning in the 1930s multinational pulp companies began to gobble up the timber limits and by the 1950s the day of the independent sawmill was over. Many towns were left to weather in the woods, but some were dismantled in conformity with licences of occupation. Some houses were torn down for lumber while others were carefully dismantled and trucked to new townsites or to lakesides to become cottages.

The railways also paved the way for mining. In some cases, such as the discovery of silver at Cobalt, the actual railway work unearthed the riches. In most cases they simply opened new territory for prospecting. The first areas to boom were the silver fields west of Thunder Bay and the Seine River and Manitou gold fields near the Manitoba border.

Ontario's early northwestern gold rushes had been marred by barroom brawls, smuggling and phoney claims. By the 1930s the frontier-type towns had disappeared and prospecting changed. While all the old excitement resurfaced, gold exploration was more scientific and, under the auspices of larger mining companies, more organized. In fact the 1930s gold rush was downright civilized.

The airplane age opened parts of Ontario which had been inaccessible. During the 1920s and 30s their mineral potential began to show and three major gold fields were uncovered.

In the barren plateau north of Lake Superior's shoreline appeared the Longlac gold field with its 17 mines and townsites. Of these Bankfield and Leitch became the largest, supporting schools, stores, churches and sports teams. Hardrock, the original railside boom town, was quickly replaced by Geraldton which remains today the area's busy regional centre.

Smaller rushes opened the Pickle Lake and Red Lake areas. Despite a complicated transportation system of lakes and portages, the Pickle Lake field gave birth to three sizeable towns: Pickle Crow, Central Patricia and Pickle Lake. By 1966 Pickle Crow was totally vacated, Central Patricia partly so, but Pickle Lake was endowed with a tourist boom which allowed it to weather the death of the gold field.

The Red Lake field was widely dispersed. So remote were some of its mines and townsites that they remained accessible only by air. The boom lasted only two decades and by 1960 most of the 13 mines had shut down. Uchi and Berens River, the largest of the distant towns were self-sustaining and despite the passage of three decades, retain most of their townscapes. Casummit, Lingman and Jackson-Manion, likewise abandoned, were little more than mining camps. Red Lake and Madsen however, subsequently obtained highway access and have become busy recreational and logging centres.

Most mining camps remained small, comprising a couple of bunkhouses while a few mushroomed into large townsites. Often the deposits were small and quickly ran dry; others were deep and produced for several decades. When the mills fell silent the buildings were moved to other towns or simply abandoned.

The final blow fell in the 1950s and 60s when an ambitious program of highway construction shifted the focus away from railways completely. The ghost towns of the north are Ontario's best. Most are less than 50 years old, their buildings firm. Remoteness has usually protected them from vandalism. While a few have vanished and a few badly deteriorated, most remain haunting and photogenic. The journeys to them are well worth the effort.

JACKFISH

Of Ontario's northern ghost towns, Jackfish is one of the the best, yet it lies just five kilometers (3 miles) from the Trans Canada Highway. Its structures are solid, its beach sandy and the view over Lake Superior spectacular.

The Jackfish story predates even the first railways. In the 1870s the Dahls, Hendricksons and Almos, perhaps seeing some of their native Scandinavia in Superior's windswept northeastern shoreline, settled in a sheltered harbour called Jackfish Bay. Here they thought they could fish undisturbed.

In 1884 the tranquillity of their new homeland was shattered by the railway. As the construction crews surged forward, the CPR threw together a construction town with a dock, hotel and a scattering of frame and log cabins. At the docks ships would unload everything from ties to kerosene to flour and meat. There were three dynamite factories run by the railways assembling the dangerous substance from chemicals brought by ship. The dynamite was used to blast the railbed through northern Ontario's bedrock.

Crammed with restless railroaders, Jackfish was rowdy and lawless. The situation was so bad in 1885 that the *Port Arthur Weekly Herald* ran

Even before CPR built its mighty coal docks, Jackfish was an active fishing village.

101

The earliest buildings at Jackfish were those belonging to the fishermen and the railway construction crew. Notice on the far left a crowd of people and what appears to be the stern of a steamer.

a feature on the thriving trade in whiskey, gambling and the shadowy figures who ran the underworld. One was Ed McMartin.

In November of 1885 McMartin suddenly appeared in James McKay's boarding house looking for a man by the name of Merrit who was trying to move in on McMartin's exclusive bootlegging and gambling action. McKay tried to throw McMartin out, but a brawl erupted and McMartin bit off McKay's finger. While McKay howled in pain McMartin fled into the night and hopped a departing freight train.

He didn't go far, probably because he wanted to keep an eye on his illegal operations in Jackfish. In January of 1886, 200 kilometers (125 miles) east in Cartier, the railroad police caught up with McMartin. They took no chances. When McMartin resisted arrest, they shot and killed him.

Although ramshackle and temporary, the town was just the start of CPR's interest in Jackfish Bay. Attracted by the deep sheltered water, the CPR started using the town as a transshipment point for Pennsylvania coal bound for the railway's divisional points of Chapleau and Cartier. They erected a 600-foot trestle dock and added boarding houses and family dwellings. The railway then hired 300 men to operate the two towering cranes and the coal cars. In the storage yards a few meters away 600,000 tons of coal formed hills 12 meters high. During the navigation season activity went on around the clock.

The Scandinavian fishing families prospered with the town. With readily available transportation they were able to pack trout and whitefish into 200-pound boxes and ship them to the St. Lawrence Fish Market in Montreal from their summer fishing village on the nearby Slate Islands.

Led by these two industries, Jackfish enjoyed its prime years from 1900 to 1940. Scattered over the hilly shore were the general store, two churches, a school and 30 houses. By the tracks were the station, water tower, six CP houses and coal facilities. On the sand next to the wharf sat net sheds, an ice house and the fishermen's beached mackinaws— flat-bottomed, double-ended boats indigenous to the northern Great Lakes.

In 1893 William Fraser built the Lakeview Hotel. It was constructed originally to house the seasonal workers but soon expanded. Sailors, townsfolk and the railwaymen would crowd the Lakeview's taproom. There the dances usually lasted until 3 a.m. and the steam whistles on departing freighters often screeched at first light to call carousing sailors back from the Lakeview to a departing ship.

In the 30s a wave of tourism swept over the shore of Superior. Southerners came to marvel at the wild mountains and valleys of the Superior shoreline, among them the famous painters, "The Group of Seven". CPR brochures boasted about the angling and Jackfish soon became the site of an annual fishing derby.

Jackfish was also famous for its pebbles. Made smooth and round by Superior's ceaseless waves, the hard beach pebbles were perfect for grinding. From 1911 to 1915 the Whelan Company of Port Arthur employed 40 men to bag the pebbles for grinding limestone to cement

One of the larger buildings at Jackfish was a railway bunkhouse built to accommodate the coal crews.

at the Canada Cement Company in Montreal. During the same time the C.W.Cox Timber Company towed logs to the Jackfish wharf where they were loaded onto ships destined for Green Bay, Wisconsin.

Jackfish residents realized the village was doomed in the 1940s when the CPR began to switch from steam to diesel locomotive and didn't need coal. In 1948 Jackfish watched the last coal freighter steam away from the dock. By 1964 the lamprey eel had so devastated the Lake Superior fishery that Jackfish's fishermen wound their nets and hauled their boats ashore for the last time. The churches, school and station closed and in the 60s the Lakeview Hotel burned to the ground. A handful of residents lingered to live out a few years of their retirement in familiar surroundings, but when they had departed Jackfish stood empty, its eight decades only a memory.

Ten kilometers (6 miles) east of Terrace Bay, the Trans Canada Highway passes within walking distance of Jackfish. Although the rushing motorists ignore the site, each summer a few residents return to fish or relive old memories. Here they see the old houses disappearing slowly behind saplings and tall grass, the boat hulls rotting on the beach. They can walk among the cracking concrete ruins of the coal facilities, a vestige of the age of steam which caused the boom and bust of this intriguing ghost town.

NICHOLSON

The little Nicholson Catholic church is quiet now. Its roof is sagging, its steeple tilts. Wind and rain have long ago removed its paint and the wood has turned a rusty brown. In the tall grasses around the church scattered cabins share the same fate.

By 1870 the lumbermen had mowed down Ontario's southern forests and set their sights on the north. There, beyond reach of the river highways, lay wide stands of prime pine, tantalizing but inaccessible.

In the 1880s when the first of the railways sliced through the remote woodlands it brought men, money and mill towns. Railside mill towns replaced those on the shoreline. Among the larger were Nicholson, Dalton and Tionaga.

Nicholson was created by two men of modest beginnings. The Canadian Pacific Railway reached Chapleau in 1886 and brought with it engineer George Nicholson. A year later James Austin opened a general store. One of the CPR's insatiable construction demands was for ties. Austin sensed profit and hired several French-Canadian lumbermen to handcut ties. By 1900 Austin and Nicholson had become close friends and on a CPR siding beside Windermere Lake 20 kilometers (12 miles)

Nicholson's Catholic church today casts a lonely silhouette.

These two photos (see top of page 107) show a panorama of the village of Nicholson. The store and school are in the foreground, the Austin and Nicholson homes on the point of land in the left foreground.

These two dilapidated Nicholson homes are barely hanging on. The building in the foreground shows the construction method of some of the old homes: horizontal planks with vertical boards nailed on top.

See photo at top of page 106.

west of Chapleau, they began producing ties. An extensive highway of lakes and rivers allowed them to tap prime pine stands which could be floated to the siding for cutting and loading.

The early Austin and Nicholson years were quiet. At first they constructed only a small mill, bunkhouse, cookery and manager's house. The CPR towed in a railway car to serve as a station. By 1910 Austin and Nicholson had acquired a 3,200-square-kilometer (2,000-square-mile) addition to their timber limits. They enlarged their mill and for $56 purchased from the government the rest of the peninsula for the townsite they called Nicholson.

The town boomed. Facing the railway siding which curved into the crescent-shaped peninsula were the company store, school, Sheffield's boarding house, a row of cabins and the town's social centre—Pottney's pool room. A two-storey station replaced the railway car. Across the tracks stood an Anglican church, while on a hill were the grand homes of Austin and Nicholson. Later the partners added a theatre and behind their executive homes, a tennis court. The residents also enjoyed a post office, free grocery delivery, electricity and police protection.

The *Canadian Lumberman and Woodworker*, a trade publication, paid strict attention to the accommodation offered transient lumbermen, trying to lure them to the remote towns. Nicholson was highly regarded with a two-storey bunkhouse containing 68 bunkbeds and a grand total of 24 spittoons.

On most Saturday nights Nicholson came to life with square dancing in the school, but the folks at Nicholson especially looked forward to the nights Omer Lauzon came to town.

Omer was a quiet, sallow man who dressed like an undertaker. Every

107

Main Street at Nicholson was the railway siding. Four of the buildings shown in this photo, including the Catholic church still survive.

Nicholson's Catholic church began life as the school house. It dominates the meadow where many of the other buildings once stood.

few weeks he climbed off the train with his huge, clacking projector and a stack of the latest Hollywood silent movies. With his sheaf of music ready for any pianist who would play during the movie, Lauzon had a regular circuit of mill towns eager to pack local halls for his movies.

Anyone with a wish for stronger entertainment clambered aboard the train for Chapleau, where the livier attractions of liquor and ladies awaited them.

For 20 years Nicholson bustled as a permanent family town. A new two-storey school replaced the first school which became the Catholic church. There was only a small number of Protestants because most of the lumbermen were French-Canadian. Indeed the existence of an Anglican church came as a surprise to the Bishop of Algoma. "You imply the existence of a church," he wrote to a student priest in Nicholson. "If there is a church I would be obliged if you would kindly send me a brief description of it in order that it may be entered in our books."

The mill itself was widely acclaimed. Operating in two daily ten-hour shifts it had, by 1924, produced an unmatched 2½-million railway ties, enough for over 2,500 kilometers (1,500 miles) of railway track. The Austin-Nicholson empire burgeoned and soon dominated northeastern Ontario. By 1930 they had added new mills and created new towns along the CP line at Sulton, Devon, Dalton and Bertrand, but Nicholson's days were numbered.

Ontario's railway boom had slowed down and the demand for ties dwindled. The mill turned to supplying timber and pulpwood to the steel and pulp mills in Sault Ste. Marie.

Then in 1933 the Nicholson mill, the lifeblood of the town, burned

From the foundation of the Nicholson railway station, cottagers flag down the mighty transcontinental train. The ghost town of Nicholson is still a flag stop.

down. Rather than replace the mill, the company simply amalgamated operations with those in Dalton. Suddenly Nicholson had no reason to exist. Although the company offered residents their homes for $25, most moved on. From a population peak of 800, Nicholson plummeted to 25, mostly trappers and railway section men. In 1936 the school house closed and was replaced by a "mobile school" which was towed in by train one week in four. The store survived until 1956, the station a couple of years longer. By 1960 Nicholson was a ghost town and next to Depot Harbour, Ontario's largest.

In 1975 the Ontario Ministry of Culture and Recreation prepared an exhaustive study of the Austin-Nicholson empire and of the town of Nicholson. It was, they felt, the best example of a company mill town which had played such a vital role in northern Ontario's history and as such should be protected. The government, however, ignored the recommendations and since then rot, snow loads and arson have claimed many of the buildings.

For those who wish to board Via Rail's Budd car in Chapleau, the single-car train will take them the 20 kilometers (12 miles) to Windermere Lake. The dozen or so surviving structures remain a photographer's dream and an explorer's delight. In the best northern tradition you'll have to flag the train down for the return journey.

DALTON and DALTON STATION

In the 1920s Nicholson was basking in its heyday and the Austin-Nicholson empire expanding. The growth led to an additional mill at the new town of Dalton Mills. In 1920 George Nicholson successfully pleaded with Albert Grigg, Ontario's Deputy Minister of Lands and Forests for larger limits and an unprecedented 2,462-acre townsite. "We of course recognize that this is a comparatively large area," he wrote, "but the peculiar location makes it necessary in order that the operation be carried out safely and successfully." The peculiar location was a narrows on the Shakwamkwa River. The flat sandy peninsulas which pinched the river were ideal construction sites.

In 1921 Austin and Nicholson built the most advanced mill of the day. "The equipment of the mill is in every way modern," observed the *Canadian Lumberman and Woodworker* in October, 1922. "Much of the heavy work is done away with. The transferring of ties or lumber is all done by foot pedals." At first Dalton Mills claimed only six dwellings and two bunkhouses, but within two years it had boomed into a thriving town.

Dalton Mills provided the workers with facilities unheard-of in Ontario's other rugged lumber camps. Besides indoor toilets and electricity, the lumbermen enjoyed two lanes of bowling, five pool tables, an ice cream parlour and a movie theatre. In the Plaza Theatre, wrote the *Canadian Lumberman and Woodworker* "there was always a full house and there was always a rush for the ice cream parlour after the show." Clearly Dalton Mills was no average lumber camp. By 1923 it could claim two

One of Dalton's donkey engines rusts on a disused siding. The narrow-gauge rails needed for these logging engines could be quickly laid right to the bush where operations were going on.

111

Dalton's huge bunkhouse contained 100 bedrooms and had indoor plumbing.

Dalton Station contains many empty buildings that have only recently been abandoned.

churches, a store and 36 houses. The two-storey bunkhouse contained 100 bedrooms each complete with bed, table, bench and spittoon. A butcher shop with a freezer, kept the town supplied with fresh meat. By 1927 more than 80 buildings clustered on the two riverbanks and made Dalton Mills one of the largest towns in northeastern Ontario.

While the town covered the west bank of the river, the mill and its buildings lay across the wooden bridge on the eastern bank. Five kilometers (three miles) north at Dalton Station on the CPR main line lay the Austin loading yards. The station, railway section house and a handful of houses became the focus for the next phase of Dalton Mills' lumbering history.

Dalton Mills survived its first mill fire in 1939, but when the mill burned again in 1949 the Austin Lumber Company (Nicholson had retired in 1934) abandoned the site. A newer mill at Bertrand 90 kilometers (55 miles) west satisfied all demand. Austin's licence of occupation dictated that all buildings be removed from the site, so homes were burnt, moved or simply collapsed into a ghostly rubble.

In 1956 the W. Plaunt Company of Sudbury purchased the Austin Company and in 1962 shut the Bertrand mill. It opened a new electric mill at Dalton Station and for a time the new Dalton was as busy as the old. Its station, church, school, mill, gas station and a dozen homes lined a network of dirt streets beside the track. Fire, again, destroyed the mill and halted the town's growth for a third and final time.

The scars are still fresh. Several homes stand gaunt and empty as do the galvanized walls of the mill. The church is now used only as a seasonal residence while the gas pumps sit rusting. Despite the recent construction of Highway 651, which passes within meters of Dalton Station 100 kilometers (60 miles) west of Chapleau, the village remains one of the north's more recent ghost towns. Meanwhile, time and the forest have claimed most of old Dalton Mills. The bridge cribbing still crosses the river narrows, two houses, part of the boarding house and the church steeple still stand on the western shore. On the eastern shore a line of now rail-less ties, machinery and foundations lie amid a young poplar stand.

The log bridge that connected the village homes at Dalton to the mill.

113

TIONAGA

Most of the lumber and mining camps which served as internment camps for Japanese Canadians in this country's most shameful act of WWII were in the interior of British Columbia, but one of Northern Ontario's ghost towns also bears the taint of this wartime cruelty: Tionaga.

British Columbia businessmen and politicians, uneasy over the entry of Japan into World War II, persuaded Liberal Prime Minister Mac-Kenzie King to inter Japanese Canadians because they feared they would act treasonably. With rapacious greed, the businessmen bought up Japanese-Canadian holdings at fire-sale prices as the Japanese were moved away from the Pacific coast and into abandoned towns. Most were taken to the interior of B.C. or the Prairies, but some were forced to make the long trip to Northern Ontario and Tionaga.

Tionaga had begun life 20 years earlier as a siding and station on the new Canadian Northern Railway. The Acme Timber and Lumber Company quickly built a tie mill at the siding and dotted the region with lumber camps. Tie-making flourished. In 1934 Ben Merwin reorganized Acme, changed the name to Pinelands and led Tionaga into its boom years. He built a new planing mill and added warehouses, a school and 25 wooden cabins. Both CN and the Ontario Department of Lands and Forests opened headquarters for their staff and crew. As its population soared to 300, Tionaga added a post office, store and an infirmary tended by a nurse and visited twice a month by a doctor.

The site was less than ideal. Jagged rock ridges hemmed in the tracks on both sides. Perched awkwardly on the granite rocks above, the buildings were linked by narrow footpaths. The 30s also heralded a boom in mining. The railway had suddenly opened a large section of northeastern Ontario to exploration and more than 17 mining companies sent prospectors along the rivers and into the hills. Only a few struck it rich.

Just three and a half kilometers (two miles) west of Tionaga a barite pit operated for a few years. Barite, a soft opaque crystal, is used as a filler in paint and in oil drilling. Miners sorted the sharp stones, heaved them into a wagon which straining horses tugged along a wagon road to Tionaga for shipment. Hollinger Consolidated Gold Mining Company hauled supplies along the same road for barging to its short-lived Smith Thorne gold operation 30 kilometers (18 miles) away on Horwood Lake.

While Tionaga diversified, Pinelands moved its tie operations to Shawmere, 50 kilometers (30 miles) away. The Pinelands' buildings at Tionaga stood empty until the screaming raid on Pearl Harbour signalled Japan's entry into the second World War. The old Pinelands site, with its structurally sound cabins became home to 30 uprooted Japanese-Canadian families for the duration of the war.

The Japanese left little mark on the village. No record exists to tell what relations, if any, they had with the local population. At the end of

The Pinelands' logging camp on Horwood Lake near Tionaga has survived in unusually good condition. The nearly impassable road leading to the site has helped keep vandals away.

the war they were set free to go home... but there were no homes to go to. Many took what work they could; a few even took in laundry, several joined Pinelands when the company moved back to the Tionaga area in the late 40s. Other former internees have risen to responsible positions in Northern Ontario.

Pinelands moved back into the former Acme lumber camp on nearby Horwood Lake. There it opened a year-round sawmill and added an office, tuck shop, garage, cookery, bunkhouse, pool hall and a dozen log cabins. The new town boomed and quickly surpassed Tionaga.

Both towns were still living on borrowed time. By 1949 the mines were shut and in 1953 Pinelands closed its Horwood Lake mill. In the same year the Ontario Department of Lands and Forests closed its headquarters and ten years later the CNR moved its large wooden railway station eight kilometers (5 miles) west. Once the hub of the northeast, Tionaga stood silent and empty.

Gradually the sagging cabins fell victims to vandalism, fire and snow loads. Today only two remain: the school and a cabin. On Horwood Lake, four kilometers (2½ miles) west, Pinelands' little mill town stands unaltered. The solid log cabins, bunks and cookery line the main street, hardly changed from the day the loggers left. The mill has gone—moved to Timmins—but the rusting cone-shaped sawdust burner still stands. The site lies south of Highway 101, east of Folyet at the end of an eight-kilometer (5-mile) jeep road that is punishing and often impassable. It is far easier and almost as fast to hike in, for the reward at road's end is the northeast's only logging camp to survive the dual ravages of weather and intruders intact.

TOPHET

"The need to obtain a reserve is urgent," stressed a 1946 Indian Affairs Branch report, "(The Indians) are scattered around the district and in their present locations cannot be given adequate supervision. Their progress is being retarded and it seems desirable that they should be located on the reserve where health and educational facilities can be available... include this scattered group in our post war slum clearing program." So Tophet on the CPR became their designated new home. When the highways replaced the railways, it was abandoned to become the northeast's largest Indian ghost town.

The Cree of northeastern Ontario were by nature nomads. Since moving into the region countless generations before, they had always travelled the lakes and rivers in pursuit of game and fish.

With the arrival of the railways and of lumbering, many Cree exchanged the uncertainty of hunting for the white man's wage and his store-bought food. Their simple cabins formed shanty towns on the outskirts of the white man's villages with such names as Nissan, Franz, Elsas, Peterbell and Oba. In 1946, with the war over, Ottawa's Indian Affairs Branch embarked on what it called "northern slum clearance", a noble phrase which meant herding the bands onto reserves. They approached L. B. MacDougall, the new Deputy Minister of Ontario's Department of Lands

Although Tophet was a railway village its residents could travel via rough logging roads to Chapleau.

A touching reminder of the days when Tophet was home to two dozen Cree families.

and Forests with a plan to resettle the particularly hard-pressed Brunswick House band.

Under the plan the federal government would buy from the province a Crown township, one of the hundreds which Ontario owned, and gather the scattered Brunswick House band together on it. The Cree were equally anxious to regain the fishing and hunting grounds they had lost in 1938 when Ontario acquired the extensive Chapleau Game Preserve and readily entered into negotiations. Problems arose when the Cree and Ontario negotiators failed to agree on which townships should comprise the new reserve. The federal government ended the wrangling on November 13, 1947, by purchasing a compromise township, Mountbatten, for $5,000.

The nagging problem of employment was also quickly solved. A lumber company with the improbable name of Kalamazoo Vegetable and Parchment Company (KVP) retained timber rights to Mountbatten. A. H. Bruk, KVP's woodlands manager, assured the government, "We have no objection to the band being established on the reserve.... We would be glad to have the Indians produce wood for us and we would be prepared to look after the installation of loading spurs."

Buoyed by the prospect of game and jobs, the Brunswick House Cree left behind their scattered shanty towns and gathered on their new homeland. In 1950 they created a 25-lot subdivision, the 30×50-meter (100×150-foot) lots fronting cross-like on two roads and each soon sprouted a sturdy white frame house. Special lots of 100×76 meters

117

(300 × 250 feet) were set aside for a school and a warehouse. Most importantly the CPR gave the reserve accessibility. Only a few crude bush roads crisscrossed the north and the railway was the lifeline and only outside link for the area's villages. The nearby CPR station gave this village its name, Tophet.

While KVP prospered the Indians had jobs. In 1955 the company lost its cutting rights and many Cree lost their incomes. A few worked for the railway, some trapped, many turned to welfare; others simply moved away from the reserve. Within ten years Tophet's population plunged from 180 to 70.

The 1960s were a road-building decade for northeastern Ontario. Highway 101 had pushed through the woods linking Chapleau, Timmins and Wawa and overnight the railway villages became obsolete. Tophet was suddenly a backwater. Chief Fred Neshawabin decided that the only way to regroup his band and restore prosperity would be to move again.

In 1972 Neshawabin concluded a land exchange. For 640 acres on Highway 101 adjacent to Chapleau, he would surrender an equal amount from the southwest corner of the reserve. In 1973 the Duck Lake Indian Reserve was opened and for the first time the Indians enjoyed electricity and pressurized water systems. Their children could now be bussed daily to the secondary school in Chapleau rather than board away from their families during the winters. The railway and lumber companies of Chapleau offered ample jobs.

Meanwhile Tophet was left to rot. Of the 25 homes only a half dozen still stand, the remainder reduced to charred foundations. There are countless uncharted Indian ghost towns throughout Northern Ontario. One, Summer Beaver, sprung back to life recently when the Cree decided to return, to get away from the very things the Duck Lake Indians were seeking.

Many of Neshawabin's men do return and hunt on the reserve and keep the road to Tophet open. It leaves Highway 129 about 30 kilometers (18 miles) south of Chapleau and winds for 10 kilometers (6 miles) to the town, the largest and most accessible of northeastern Ontario's abandoned Cree villages.

SILVER CENTRE

The Lorrain Valley Road winds south from Cobalt through a hidden valley and ends at the mouth of the mighty Montreal River. On a side trail a young forest is advancing around the headframes and the shells of one of the Cobalt area's once-famous silver towns: Silver Centre.

It began, not with prospectors, but with two timber scouts. In 1903 lumber king J. R. Booth sent J. H. McKinley and Ernest Darragh to cruise the Lake Temiskaming forests for tie timber. On August 7, on the shores of Cobalt Lake, a shimmer of light from a rock caught their eye.

"In washing some of the gravel in the lake," McKinley later recounted, "there were flakes or leaves of a bright colour which we could bend. I immediately thought of the old forty-niner and placed a piece between my teeth and I succeeded in marking it very easily." T. W. Gibson of the Ontario Bureau of Mines confirmed the find: silver.

The news at first brought only a yawn, but when carloads of rich ore rumbled out, the rush was on. Within a year, 16 mines were tunnelled into the rocky hills. By 1910 that figure had tripled and 55 mines pulled $17.5 million in silver from the ground, equal to five dollars worth of silver for every person in the country. Clinging to the hillside by the lake, a village named Cobalt boomed to 10,000 people, its streets lined with solid homes and sturdy brick stores.

Flushed with the success of the Cobalt finds, prospectors tramped further afield. In 1907, amid the spectacular peaks overlooking Lake Tem-

Silver Centre's hotel (left) and mine office were the centre of this now vanished silver boom town.

The first village to be called Silver Centre was located not at the mines, but at a government townsite by the landing on Lake Temiskaming.

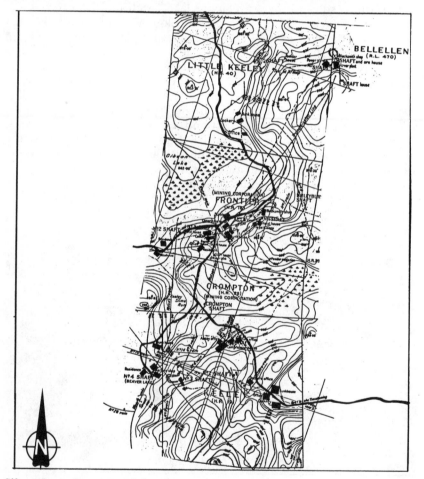

Silver Centre's scattered development is clearly shown on this 1920s Ontario government mining map.

iskaming 30 kilometers (18 miles) south of Cobalt, prospectors Bob Jowsey, Charles Keeley and James Woods struck more silver. Woods and Keeley staked the claim and the following spring they found that the rock contained an unusually rich 1,000 ounces of silver per ton of ore. So began Silver Centre.

Near the wharf on Lake Temiskaming, the only access to the discovery, the Ontario government surveyed two townsites with the names "66" and "Lorrain City". When the post office opened, it ignored the government and took the more colourful name Silver Centre. Though little more than a tent and shack village, it could claim a restaurant run by the Pickerings and a store operated by the Provenchers. Bill Bulger of Haileybury provided the community's only outside link with his daily summer steamer service. From the landings, Joe Coates urged his horse teams over roads full of pot-holes carrying freight and passengers to the noisy mines eight kilometers (five miles) inland. As the mine camps grew, the post office moved inland and the landing townsites were abandoned.

Of Silver Centre's first half-dozen mining attempts only two flourished. One was Keeley's mine, which between 1909 and 1912 produced 24,000 ounces of silver. Then his creditor, the Farmer's Bank, declared bankruptcy and an Almonte geologist, Dr. MacIntosh Bell acquired the mine. Six years and a war would pass before Bell would rejuvenate the faltering town.

The Wettlaufer Mine was more prosperous for it lay on a larger deposit. In its first six years the Wettlaufer yielded a staggering two-and-one-half-million ounces of silver. The remaining mines with names like Maidens, Bellellen, Frontier and Currie were disappointments and short-lived. After 1914 the silver market slumped and took with it the promising

During the Cobalt silver rush certain essential facilities were hurriedly established. Regal beer was just one of hundreds of locally brewed beers across Ontario which have sadly disappeared. Canadian beer is worse-off for the absence of their unique tastes.

Although long since abandoned, many of the Silver Centre mines have left a legacy of mine buildings and headframes.

little town. Activity was sporadic and limited to drilling or tailing work until, in 1920, MacIntosh Bell breathed life back into Silver Centre. After paying off the Farmer's Bank debts he set out to rediscover the rich Woods' vein. He restarted the Keeley and Frontier mines and Silver Centre became the boom town of the northeast. Trees were cleared to open the ground for more exploration and the rugged rockland soon resembled a moonscape. Headframes dotted the hilltops, at their feet the wooden shafthouses, offices, dining halls and bunkhouses.

Silver Centre's appearance confused many visitors for it had no organization. Development focused on the headframes while scattered buildings lined the twisting roads that connected them. While most residents were forced to live in stifling bunkhouses, a few families enjoyed the relative freedom of small cabins. Mining executives of course bathed in the luxury of substantial homes out of sight and sound of the clanging mines. Hours were long and the pay low. To offset these hardships, the townspeople plunged into sports with extra enthusiasm. Silver Centre's hockey and baseball teams won championships right across northern Ontario.

In 1924 the Temiskaming and Northern Ontario Railway opened a branch line from Cobalt and started daily service. Each weekend the passenger cars were jammed with chattering miners anxious to sample the illicit night-life of Cobalt. Cobalt, like Silver Centre, was a mining town and by law, dry, but many a back door led to dimly lit, smokey rooms where liquor flowed and painted ladies plied their trade.

Despite these palmy days, the end lay just over the horizon. By 1926 all but the Keeley and Frontier veins were dry. The population fell by half and the train service was cut to three trips a week. In 1931 the last two mines closed and the trains fell silent. Silver Centre became a ghost town. Buildings disappeared, the rails were lifted and the forest began to reclaim the site.

Today a wide gravel road plunges down the Lorrain Valley from North Cobalt and bypasses Silver Centre. The narrow, jolting road into the one-time town has not changed. In the readvancing forest loom weathered headframes, windowless warehouses and the sagging shells of what were once private homes. They are all silent reminders of the days when Silver Centre was one of Canada's leading silver towns. Fittingly, until the late 1960s, the name continued to appear on Government of Ontario road maps as if to say the town may have died, but its memory had not.

Many of Silver Centre's buildings lined the winding roads that connected the various mines.

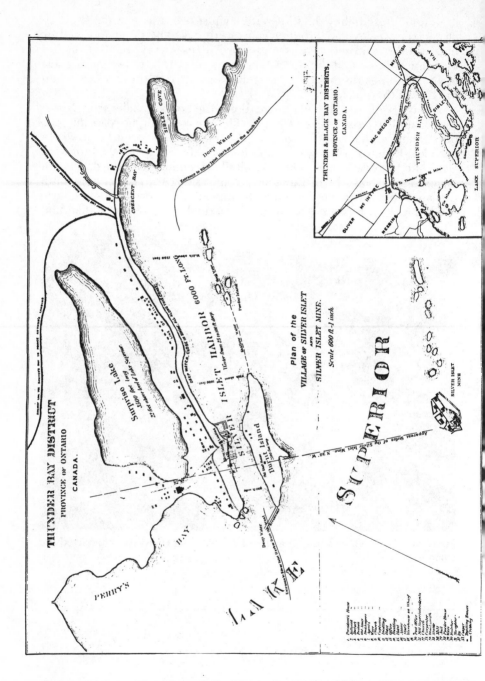

The extent of development at Silver Islet is graphically shown on this early sketch map.

124

SILVER ISLET

For millenia Skull Islet sat dwarfed beneath the ancient limestone plateau known as the Sleeping Giant. Lake Superior's grey rolling waves washed over it constantly, hiding Ontario's richest silver deposit.

In 1845 prospector Joseph Woods visited the area and struck silver, but he didn't explore what lay on the small patch of rock a few hundred feet offshore. The following year the Montreal Mining Company acquired the remote claim, but ignored it for 20 years until the Ontario government slapped a two-cent-per-acre tax on undeveloped claims.

The company dispatched Thomas MacFarlane to begin detailed survey work. In June of 1868 he met up with Gerry Brown and John Morgan who were to help him. On a quiet windless day, Brown landed on Skull Islet to plant a survey stake and noticed a silver-bearing rock. He went back to get MacFarlane and Morgan and the three paddled out. Down by the water, not far from where they had landed, John Morgan found a rock which glittered with native silver. They blasted out samples and continued their summer's work.

The following year MacFarlane returned to start the slow fight for Superior's silver, which lay in veins running out from the island under the lake. He couldn't do much beyond stopping the company from hav-

What appears to be a mirage on the horizon is the fabled Silver Islet. Originally a shoal the size of a baseball diamond, Silver Islet became North America's most prolific silver mine.

William Frue was the man who finally tamed Superior's waves and put the riches of Silver Islet into production.

A portion of the miners' mainland town at Silver Islet shortly after its construction. It has changed little.

ing to pay the two-cent tax. Waves continuously filled his shaft until winter froze the lake into submission, From the rich veins he managed to bring up $23,000 of silver ore, but he needed $50,000 for a protective cribbing to keep Superior away. The financially troubled company was forced to sell the rock to Major Alexander Sibley of Detroit for the then exorbitant sum of $225,000. It would prove to be a bargain for the Major.

As soon as the deal was completed and signed in Montreal, Sibley wired William Frue, the man who would beat Superior. Frue, of Irish descent, had already made a name for himself in mining engineering circles in Michigan. He and Sibley struck a deal. If Frue could recover silver worth the full purchase price of the mine in the first year of operation, Frue would get a $25,000 bonus.

As soon as the wire arrived Frue had his chartered steamer thrashing across the lake with supplies and a crew of 30 of his most trusted Cornish miners. The men of Cornwall, on England's western coast, had earned a reputation for mining the difficult Cornwall tin deposits. They faced an even more difficult task at Silver Islet.

Frue's picture shows a proud man with piercing eyes, but Superior must have brought him to the breaking point that first year. Although he urged his men on with production bonuses of their own, a raging October gale easily tore his first breakwater to shreds, a November storm shattered his second wall and his third barely survived the winter only to be torn away in March by the surging ice which effortlessly pushed his man-made structure into the sea. Undeterred, Frue started again and enlarged his breakwater until he had created an artificial island ten times the size of the original. With the men working double shifts and the furnaces burning deep into the night, Frue managed to dig enough silver out of the rich rock. He made the quota and earned his bonus.

When the new island could withstand all he thought Superior could hurl at it, Frue constructed a boarding house, blacksmith, engine house and shafthouse. Most critical was the boiler to pump the shaft dry, for it leaked continually. Miners streamed in from as far away as Norway because Frue hired the best and for two years silver flowed from the shafts.

In 1873 Superior struck back. A freak tidal wave loomed out of the lake and rumbled over the islet, carrying everything with it. When the icy water touched the hot boiler it exploded and killed two men. Persevering, Frue again enlarged the island and when he finished he had space to add four boarding houses, a library and a hospital.

On the mainland, a town was growing. Protected from Superior's fury by Burnt Island, a store, customs house, assay office, school, two churches, hotel and 40 houses lined the beach. Sibley's house, with its four bedrooms, billiard room and servant's quarters was the grandest of the lot. Behind the village stood the 50-stamp mill and a log jailhouse.

Coming off shift the men would grumble as they wound their way from the dock to the hotel or boarding houses for a drink. The mine was wet and dangerous and, at freeze-up and spring break-up, cut off from the mainland. Their clothes steaming from the damp mine, they huddled next to roaring stoves and sipped whiskey to bring feeling back to their numb bodies. Frue allowed miners only two drinks a day and they watched sourly as their consumption was chalked up on a board above the bar.

Despite Frue's best efforts to keep booze away from his workers, bootlegging ran rampant. The jail was designed to cope with a boisterous town and contained a bedroom for the jailer, an office, dayroom and five cells which were often occupied by those who had found a source of more alcohol. At one time or another the cells were occupied by some of the swindlers and cheats who were drawn to the area's new-found wealth. Sitting around the hotel's stove one of the tales the men told was how their boss Frue uncovered one of the best planned swindles ever attempted on Superior's north shore.

In 1871, four men from Michigan had staked a claim at Otter Head, east of Silver Islet, claiming they had found northern Ontario's first deposit of tin. They had convinced a group of Detroit financiers of their find and a new mining rush seemed about to start until Frue arrived to stake his own claims. He quickly grew suspicious and stopped to have a look at the veins the Michigan men had staked. Frue discovered they had chipped out part of a soft vein of rock and cemented in its place rich tin-bearing ore.

At Silver Islet's mill, one of Frue's inventions was at work. To recover minerals left in the residue from the stamping mills, Frue devised a "vanner" or separator, and installed 24 in the mill. The invention attained instant popularity and within years most stamp mills contained at least one "Frue Vanner".

On the island itself, the shafts inched deeper and soon stretched miles under Superior's waters. The deposits seemed limitless. When one vein ended another appeared and by 1883 the silver production had exceeded $3 million. The boiler pumped day and night to keep out the steady seepage, for if it ever failed, the shafts would immediately flood. It was at this weak point Superior aimed its next blow.

By 1883 the hills around the mainland village were stripped of trees and Silver Islet depended for its fuel on the autumn coal boat. As the fall days of 1883 grew shorter and ice began to form, the coal boat did not appear. Then the dreaded news—the boat was wedged in Superior's ice and stuck for the winter.

Frue carefully rationed what coal he had, but by March they were chopping up buildings to feed the boiler. Finally, with nothing left to burn, the boiler fire flickered and died: the shaft began to fill and Silver Islet was dead.

Grieving wives lined the beach as the miners sadly trooped home across the ice for the last time. They loaded onto sleighs what possessions they could carry and moved westward to the growing city of Port Arthur. They were certain that the village they left behind would disappear.

Or would it?

Around 1900 Port Arthur's residents began to look for recreational properties. The miner's sturdy homes, just 30 kilometers (18 miles) away

128

by water, on a scenic and pleasant beach, seemed ideal and were soon in heavy demand. Every summer for the past 80 years the ghost community has returned to life. Fanned by three books and countless articles, the summer residents take a strong pride in Silver Islet's history. They have preserved the cabins, restored the jail and assay office and erected a commemorative plaque. Gone, unfortunately are the mill, the Catholic church with its widow's walk and Major Sibley's grand house. The old store has only recently closed. On the rocky islet offshore the buildings have long since disappeared. Each year they sagged a little more, each year the waves lapped closer, until Superior totally reclaimed the island.

Easily accessible, Silver Islet village sits at the end of Highway 587, adjacent to Sibley Provincial Park. In the park are hiking trails and rock formations; in a village antique store, mining memorabilia and books on Silver Islet's history are for sale. As long as the buildings and the interest remain, Silver Islet is a ghost town unlikely to die. The mine died only because it was flooded. Superior alone knows what riches in silver still lie beneath the lake.

Although many of Silver Islet's buildings are well cared-for, the former general store has a forlorn appearance.

SILVER MOUNTAIN

For generations the local Ojibway band had carefully guarded the secret of the high forested mountain they called Shuniah Weachu. The secret was broken in 1884. Chief Joseph L'Avocat of the Nipigon band was so pleased about the marriage of his daughter to prospector Oliver Daunais he took him into his confidence and showed him the glittering streak of silver high on the windy plateau. This silver deposit, which stretched for over a mile, gave birth to two rambunctious mining towns. Both were called Silver Mountain. Both have vanished with little trace.

Before 1888 only a rugged bush road from Lake Superior wound past the mountains and through the woods to the site. Its condition was so coarse that the deposits lay undeveloped. Then, in 1888, the Duluth extension of the Canadian Northern Railway replaced the jolting trail and almost overnight mining towns blossomed where only wilderness had stood. In 1889 Elias Drake of St. Paul, Minnesota acquired the claim and began to mine the silver. He erected a blacksmith shop, mine office, boarding house and 20 log dwellings. On the hillside a noisy ten-stamp mill banged out 40 tons of ore per day. The town became known as Silver Mountain West End.

The mine and mill at Silver Mountain West End in 1899 shortly before it closed.

Silver Mountain West End was the larger of the two villages. Shown here in suits and ties are not miners, but Ontario parliamentarians on their northwestern tour of 1899.

Two kilometers (1.2 miles) east of West End stood its twin. Owned by the Silver Mountain Mining Company of Liverpool, England, East End in 1889 was a thriving village of nearly three dozen buildings. However, it was West End under the direction of mine manager William Rapsey that accounted for most of Silver Mountain's $500,000 silver production.

On May 1, 1891 Elias Drake died, and with silver prices in a slump, the mine closed. Chief mining inspector A. Slaght observed sadly in his 1892 report that of all Thunder Bay's mines, the promising West End, could have survived the depression. "The mine", he wrote, "never looked so well as when shut down." In the same year East End, along with the other Thunder Bay silver mines, fell victim to the depression and closed.

For ten years the mines slumbered until C. P. Russell, president of Lake Superior Mining Company, grabbed up both mountain mines. By 1904 his West End manager Herb Shear had added a new mill with 30 stamps and nine Frue vanners, and production soared to 80 tons a day. A new log store, office, shafthouse and several new log dwellings also appeared. Meanwhile, East End had poured out $366,000 worth of silver ore and caused Ontario mining inspector W. E. H. Carter to exclaim: "Changes have taken place in the silver situation at the mines west of Port Arthur from which it would appear that the scope of operations is likely to be greatly enlarged."

The company waxed even more optimistic in its first report: "Silver Mountain has produced in the short time that it has operated approximately 350,000 ounces of silver and, when opened up to connect with

131

Silver Mountain East End at the turn of the century was a busy miners' village of log cabins.

the East End mine, will commence the brightest and most interesting page in the history of silver mining in this district."

In 1901 the Census of Canada counted 685 miners, farmers and railway men in the Silver Mountain area.

Though production boomed, safety lagged. Inspector Carter lamented: "More than the usual degree of carelessness was found to prevail among the miners in the handling of dynamite, it being customary with some to prepare the frozen sticks for the evening blast by putting them into their boot caps and leaving them there all day."

After 1904 it became clear that Silver Mountain was in trouble. For two years there was no production. Then in 1906 Russell sold out to C. L. Hanson who constructed a new ten-stamp mill and sank several shafts. But the mountain had no more silver to give.

After the miners departed, the population plunged to fewer than 60. Gradually even the name was moved from the mines to the station on the new railway. The secret of the Indians was safe once more.

Today parts of the old Silver Mountain highway and the Canadian Northern Railway lie abandoned, replaced by Highway 588. The mysterious mountain is a striking cliff visible from the intersection of Highways 588 and 593 west of Thunder Bay. Little more than rubble marks the mountain-top sites of what were two of Ontario's promising silver towns.

MINE CENTRE

Of all Ontario's gold rushes, the Seine River rush should be remembered. Although it was short-lived, produced little gold and was fraught with corruption, it left a legacy of boom towns and frontier adventure reminiscent of the fabled Yukon gold rush. Today the remains of the camps and towns are hidden in the young forests near the pulp town of Fort Frances.

While settlement boomed in southern Ontario during the late 1800s, Ontario's far north remained a mystery. Its treasures were known only to Indians, trappers and fur traders until the lure of gold brought bold prospectors from southern settlements to this untamed wilderness. With little more than rushing rivers and rumours as their guide, a few intrepid men penetrated Ontario's northwest in search of gold.

One of the first was Archie McKellar, who struck gold in 1872 on Partridge Lake, west of Port Arthur (now Thunder Bay). Until the CPR's steel rails made freighting feasible, few paid attention to the find. When the CPR reached Rat Portage (now Kenora) and the South African gold industry collapsed, prospectors from as far away as the Yukon and California flooded in. By 1890 gold had been discovered on Lake of the Woods, the Manitou Lakes and the notorious Seine River.

The Seine River flows amid the smooth pink rocks of the Canadian

Mine Centre in 1899 was at its peak with several stores and hotels. Members of a legislative tour pose on the steps of the Mine Centre Hotel.

Following the decline of the Seine River gold field many of Mine Centre's inhabitants moved to the new Mine Centre Station, but much of it too has become a ghost town.

The Olive headframe and shafthouse are among the few mine buildings to survive from Mine Centre's mining days.

Shield near Ontario's remote borders with Manitoba and Minnesota. The vast maze of lakes and rivers created a highway network through an otherwise impenetrable wilderness. In 1890 the CPR had opened the woods as far as Winnipeg and steamers from Rat Portage chugged down Lake of the Woods and Rainy River carrying the eager prospectors to the Seine River gold fields.

Discovery followed discovery. In 1893 J. S. Campbell uncovered the Golden Crescent on Bad Vermillion Lake, while on Shoal Lake Thomas Weigund and Alexander Lochart unearthed the Foley. Doc Gardner was prowling around what would become the Olive, while an Indian was leading James Hammond to a legendary find on Sawbill Lake.

Few finds were producers. The Lucky Coon, Gold Bug, Mayflower, Emperor and the Ferguson all showed promise at first, but it was an empty promise. Other "mines" were simple frauds. Eager to cash in on the gold fever, dishonest prospectors sold worthless properties with such fancy names as the Money Maker, Sugar Loaf, Hibernian and the Lea Rosa de Ora. When the fever had finally subsided, only five mines survived: the Foley, Olive, the Sawbill/Hammond Reef, the Gold Star and the Little American.

The hub of the Seine River gold rush was Shoal Lake. Situated at the head of steamer navigation from Fort Frances, its shores witnessed the arrival of prospectors and miners and the making of millionaires. Steamer stops quickly mushroomed into boom towns. Bell City and Seine City appeared almost overnight. But, Mine Centre became the raucous centre of the gold field.

Here, where a small point of land extends into Shoal Lake, a busy town took shape. Jostling for space along the narrow peninsula were a drugstore, tailor shop, general store, school, post office, customs house, restaurant and jail. Its three busy hotels included the Rutledge (later the Caldwell), the Randolph and the Mine Centre.

With no law on the Seine River the miners and prospectors enforced a rough justice, often more appropriate than jail. It was Mine Centre that witnessed the taming of Jack the Fighter. Jack was a bar bully who enjoyed drawing unsuspecting strangers into a fight they would lose.

Sitting in a smokey bar with glasses full of the local brews, Sultana Lager, Mikado Pale Ale or the popular Regina Porter, the boys devised a way of teaching Jack the Fighter a lesson. A wire was quickly sent to a light-weight boxer from Minneapolis named Payne and the conspirators sat back quietly awaiting his arrival.

On the appointed night Jack found the barroom crowded and, to his puzzlement, many people willing to buy him a drink without being cajoled into it. When the diminutive and dapper Payne entered the Mine Centre bar, Jack thought he had another easy mark. He was somewhat perplexed when Payne refused to fight unless a space was cleared in the centre of the room, but Jack still thought the fight was his.

To Jack's astonishment, Payne easily dodged his lunging roundhouse swings while connecting with his own shuddering jabs. Bleeding and

A small class of students at the short-lived Bell City school in 1897.

staggering, Jack begged an end. It was the last time he picked a fight with a stranger.

The humbling of Jack the Fighter didn't stop there. The entire district learned about the fight from a tongue-in-cheek article in the Rainy Lake newspaper.

Other colourful residents included Chief Neverwash, Rattlesnake Bill and a prospector named Pegleg. For ten years after it had closed and lay abandoned, the Mine Centre Hotel featured Pegleg's wooden leg over the bar. Whatever bet he lost—or won—which made him turn over his leg for display above the bar is lost with Mine Centre.

Perhaps he left his leg as security and then skipped over the international border, which was only 15 kilometers (9 miles) away. Mine Centre was a haven for smugglers. To avoid paying an import tax on newly mined gold they developed clever ways of slipping it into the U.S. A common sight on the Rainy Lake steamers bound for Tower, Minnesota, was groups of stern prospectors armed and guarding a sack of "oats".

As the miners poured out gold, Mine Centre boomed. In 1899 seven new buildings went up including Bedford's barber shop and pool room and the Taylor and Cruse general store. E. Todd ran sawmills at both Mine Centre and nearby Bell City. Other main street businesses included Brechon's bakery who advertised "Bread, Cake and Pastry, Temperance Drinks and Chocolate Cigars". L. Hamel operated a dry goods store specializing in mining supplies. The *Rainy River Directory* put Mine Centre's population at 500 although most were miners who boarded at one of the hotels.

BELL CITY was Shoal Lake's other boom town. It was also built on a peninsula, just two kilometers east of Mine Centre. On its town plan of six streets and 120 lots stood Todd's sawmill, a handful of houses owned by John Kelly, J. Young, K. Reed, Ed Lyons and E. Todd, and the Pioneer Hotel. The Pioneer with its 25 rooms boasted canoes, guides, liquor and cigars, all for $1. a day. Although small, Bell City zealously promoted itself. "Ho for the Seine River goldfields", read the ad for the Pioneer Hotel in the *Rainy Lake Advertiser*, "all roads leading to Bad Vermillion Lake and Little Turtle Lake start here... all boats stop here."

In June of 1899 the attention of all Ontario focussed on Mine Centre and Bell City. A group of 30 members of the Ontario legislature flanked by 17 newsmen stepped off the steamer *Majestic* as part of a lengthy tour of what was called "the new Ontario." For two days they toured local mines and for two nights they were lavishly entertained, first in the Pioneer Hotel in Bell City, then at the Mine Centre Hotel. By the time they left, the unofficial mayor of Bell City had extracted a promise of $300 to improve the muddy streets of the "city".

The Seine River's other "cities" remained only dreams. SEINE CITY for a time had a steamer stop, a customs office and George Watson's boarding house, but in 1899 these moved to Mine Centre. TURTLE CITY on Big Turtle Lake and Chief Neverwash's CHIEF CITY were paper towns. Even though the *Rainy Lake Advertiser* described Chief City as "the best townsite location by far in the Seine River district and it bids fair to be a prosperous and growing city," it remained as it began, a steamer stop.

The outskirts of Mine Centre and the road to the Foley mine in 1899. Like other mining towns on the Canadian Shield, many of the houses were perched precariously on rocky outcrops.

A small village developed at the site of the Foley mine during the 1890s.

FOLEY was the only mine to blossom into a town. Discovered in 1893 by Thomas Weigund and Alex Lochart it had produced bullion worth $40,000 by 1898. Among the log and frame buildings which clustered on Shoal Lake five kilometers (3 miles) west of Mine Centre were Ryan's store, a hotel, a school taught by a Mr. Bradley, three boarding houses and a dozen miners' cabins. As usual, three large and pretentious homes were reserved for the manager, inspector and the president. The steamer *Wanda* connected Foley with Mine Centre and Fort Frances while a crude road linked Foley with Mine Centre and with the Olive and Golden Star mines. Other Seine River mines were little more than camps with their bunkhouses and one or two residences.

In 1903 the bubble burst and the mines ran dry. Mine Centre and Bell City were abandoned. The Canadian Northern Railway opened its new branch line eight kilometers (5 miles) from old Mine Centre just in time to save the town's name. The station took the name of the dying mining town and a road was built between the two. Many unemployed residents dragged their homes to railside. The old Mine Centre hotel, complete with Pegleg's leg, stood abandoned until 1910 when it was barged piece by piece to Fort Frances and re-erected as the Irwin Hotel. It stands to this day missing only the wooden leg above the bar. The rest of old Mine Centre and Bell City has collapsed.

Of the Seine River's gold mines, only the Olive has retained its old buildings. Amid the shells still struggling to remain upright stands the sturdy plank headframe, the only such survivor of the entire gold field.

Some of the other mines were reworked during the 30s and 40s, but their remains are sparse: rotting cabins at the Foley and Gold Star and the stone wall of the mill at the Golden Crescent. Auto access to these, the Shoal Lake boom towns, is impossible. Hiking boots or boat provide the only access. Sadly, the few remains are scarcely worth the effort. The contribution of the Seine River Rush to Ontario's ghost town history lies in its unique memories of frontier adventure and the frenzied activity created by gold fever.

The new Mine Centre Station still lives. In 1906 it claimed two hotels, one operated by John Davis and the other by Sinclair and McLean, the Miners' Supply Company and T. G. Rideaux' general store. R. Gillon surveyed a town plot and the town soon boasted 400 residents.

The town rose and fell with the railroad. Following the second war rail operation became centralized and the town dwindled. By 1976 Mine Centre Station's population had dropped to 88, its townsite derelict. Old stores and homes still stand in ghostly abandonment. In 1976 a new provincial highway was opened between Fort Frances and Thunder Bay passing through the old townsite. New retirement homes have been constructed and a new store and school stand beside the highway; Mine Centre has begun its third life.

A long tramway led from the Foley mine to the landing on Shoal Lake.

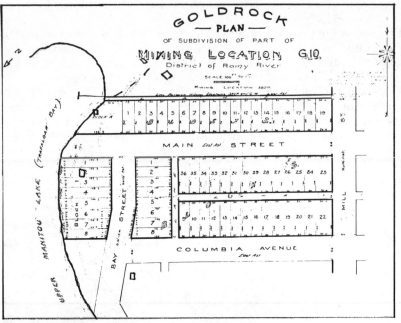

Plan of Gold Rock, 1898.

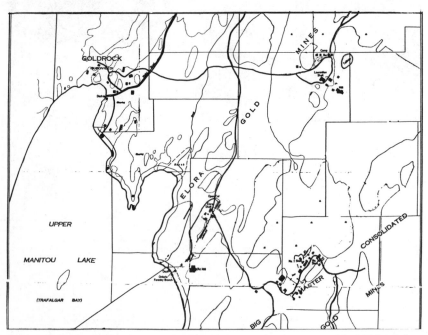

The scattered development at Gold Rock is clearly shown on this 1905 mining map.

140

GOLD ROCK

If the remnants of the Seine River rush are scanty, those left from the Manitou Lakes' rush are the most prolific of any turn-of-the-century gold town.

By 1898 northwestern Ontario's first frantic gold rush was dead. Investors fled as quickly as they had arrived when they heard of the Yukon and Klondike. But the heady Klondike fever also faded and in 1902 miners turned their eyes back to northwestern Ontario, in particular to the Manitou Lakes.

The Manitou Lakes are the largest of thousands of lakes which make a watery maze of the vast area between Fort Frances and Dryden. They had escaped unexplored during the first rush to the Seine River. Now, with the Klondike dead and gold prices rebounding, the Manitou rush began.

While dozens of diggings and discoveries dotted the shores of the Manitou Lakes the most spectacular finds were in Trafalgar Bay, a swampy inlet in the northeast corner of Upper Manitou Lake. On these shores optimistic mine owners built more than a dozen mines in the midst of which the miners added their own boisterous little town, Gold Rock.

W. A. Blackstone's Bigmaster Mine led Gold Rock into life on July 1, 1902. By November, 1901 he had completed a shafthouse, stamp mill and sawmill which cut 10,000 board feet of lumber per day. Blackstone lured miners with "high western salaries", as mining inspector Gibson referred to them and by reducing shifts to eight hours. But by the fall of 1902 the Bigmaster had produced only $5,000 worth of gold.

Gold Rock village was the focus for a dispersed group of mining camps on Manitou Lakes during the first decade of this century.

141

The **Bigmaster mill** is one of the impressive survivors at Gold Rock. Using better and more recent milling techniques the mine's tailings were re-worked in the 1930s and yielded substantial amounts of gold.

Ice conditions and lack of wood in the winter of 1903 forced the Bigmaster to close for six months. Meanwhile the ore reserves were running low and, after a period high-grading, irate stockholders foreclosed on Blackstone. High-grading involved the removal of the best gold-bearing ore as it came out of the mine and was an all-too-common practice.

Then there was Anthony Blum. In August, 1902 he bought the 20th Century claim and started mine operations almost within sight of Blackstone. On his visit in 1903 mining inspector Gibson described Blum's camp as "a collection of log and frame buildings including an office and assay office, boarding and bunkhouses, a warehouse, a stable and an ice house." From the sawmill Blum cut over 100,000 feet of lumber for the erection of a 20-stamp mill.

Just as Blum was ready to start up his new mill he discovered a still richer claim. He moved the mill to this new site and the Laurentian quickly became Gold Rock's leading producer. In addition to the mill and other mine buildings the Laurentian boasted a laboratory, electrically-lit houses and a telephone line to the Canadian Pacific Railway. The Bigmaster mining community remained the largest in the area, boasting a manager's house, boarding house, cookery and several log cabins, as well as the mill and mine buildings.

The heart of the mines was the little village of Gold Rock that grew up at the Manitou landing. In 1898 Henry Cowan laid out a townsite with 63 lots on four streets. Gold Rock boomed from a "small village of tents with a log house or two" (Ontario mining inspector Bow in 1897) to a prosperous community featuring a store, hotel, school, oil storage shed, stables and several private dwellings. The *Union Publishing Company*

142

Business Directory for 1906 listed Rowan and Martin as the store operators and W. M. York as the hotelier.

Rocky wagon roads wound from the village through the woods to the scattered mining camps. Frame and log cabins dotted the roadsides, while the boarding houses and managers' homes clustered around the head-frames. It was a loosely-knit community that numbered 500 at its peak.

Gold Rock's link with the outside was never anything more than an 11-kilometer (7-mile) logging road. It lurched through swamps and over outcrops northeasterly to Lake Minnehaha where steamers shuttled miners and supplies to the boom town of Wabigoon on the CPR.

Most of Gold Rock's mines were small and short-lived. The Little Master, located on an extension of the Bigmaster vein, shafted in 1903 and then closed temporarily in 1904 and 1905. In 1906, after another burst

A view of Gold Rock's Laurentian mill (1910) and shafthouse; the latter still stands after eight decades of neglect.

The log bunkhouse and cookery of the Laurentian mine at Gold Rock still survive in fair shape.

143

Gold Rock's hotel and store when the village was a major gold producer. On the one-storey building attached to the side of the main building there are crooked stove pipes going up from the chimney so the stove flue had enough draw to keep the fires going.

of activity, the power house burned and the Little Master closed for good.

Beside the Bigmaster and Little Master stood the Paymaster. Owned by Northern Development of Detroit, the Paymaster opened in 1906 with a work force of just 15. When Inspector Gibson warned superintendent Manley that the boiler and compressor were too close to the shafthouse, Northern Development closed down rather than pay for the change.

A neighbour of the Paymaster was the Detola. It began operations in 1906 under the ownership of the Detola Development Company. Manager Dryden Smith, who also managed the Laurentian, oversaw a work force of 25. "At the mine proper the buildings consist of a boiler and engine house, blacksmith, shafthouse, dry house and store house," remarked mines inspector A. L. Parsons in 1910. "There is also a comfortable house for the manager which is combined with the boarding house and at a short distance is a lodging house for the miners." He praised the Detola's appearance unlike Inspector Gibson did with the Paymaster: "Everything about the property is well kept and every provision seems to have been made for safety and reasonable comfort." Like the others, the Detola soon ran out of ready gold.

The big blow came when, without warning, the Laurentian ran dry. Its operators had been secretly high-grading the reserves and, with the best ore gone, they walked away. Its closing heralded Gold Rock's demise. Mining inspector Gibson wrote, "The closing down of this property, which was considered by the public the mainstay of the district, is unfortunate as it retards the investment of capital in other properties and discourages other companies from attempting to develop paying mines."

After 1911 Gold Rock sank rapidly. Its post office closed, its residents moved and its buildings decayed.

144

In the 1930s the depression caused a flurry of speculation at Gold Rock. Four old mine sites were reworked, but only the Bigmaster yielded gold. In 1942 it poured Gold Rock's first gold brick in 35 years and continued producing until February, 1948. Then silence descended once more.

The survival of so many of Gold Rock's buildings over eight decades makes it one of the province's most remarkable ghost towns. Although the old hotel, store and a few dwellings were demolished for a fishing camp, several other buildings stand, particularly those at the mine sites. The school remained intact until 1972, its books still in place on the desks. Sadly, local vandals removed the books, the desks and finally the building itself. Two kilometers (1.2 miles) from the townsite, beside the old wagon road, a small miners' cemetery lies hidden in the woods.

The Laurentian, Detola and Bigmaster mines all retain their mills. They loom above the regenerating forest, their boards weathered, the wind howling through their gaunt shells. At the Laurentian, the log boarding house and cookery survive along with shops, offices and storehouses.

An eight-kilometer (5-mile) tote road from Lake Minnehaha to the Bigmaster replaced the original lumber road in 1942. Today it still gives foot access to the one-time village from Highway 502, 50 kilometers (30 miles) south of Dryden.

An Ontario government report by archaeologists and architects described Gold Rock as unique and recommended preservation of the site. Tragically, the government has ignored these recommendations and left the fate of this extensive ghost town to the whims of vandals and nature.

A miner's cabin half-standing on the trail between Laurentian and Gold Rock village has seen better days.

BURCHELL LAKE

One hundred and sixty kilometers (95 miles) west of Thunder Bay on Highway 11-71, an arrow points to Highway 802. This secondary road winds through a readvancing forest and ends abruptly at a three-meter (10-foot) high chain link fence. Beyond the gate lies the recent ghost town of Burchell Lake, one of Ontario's best.

The site has lured prospectors for more than 100 years. In 1876 three prospectors named McNaughton, McMillan and McFee were the first to discover copper, but not until 1901, when the Ontario and Rainy River Branch of the Canadian Northern Railway finally opened the area, could production begin. In that year W. G. Pollock of the New York and Canadian Copper Company with a work force of just 14 produced 768,000 pounds of copper worth $30,700. Initially working from only a simple office and a few boarding houses, he subsequently added in 1913 another office and near the shores of the placid Burchell Lake a kilometer away, several log dwellings. He called his mine the Tip Top. However, copper prices slumped and high shipping costs forced him to close.

During the Great War, soaring copper prices re-ignited interest in the property and a narrow-gauge railway siding was built. For two years the mine churned out 45 tons of ore per day, but the rejuvenation was short-lived. The war ended, copper prices tumbled again and the Tip Top fell

Four substantial log rowhouse dwellings around 1905 when the Coldstream mine at Burchell Lake was known as Tip Top.

A crudely constructed siding gave the Tip Top mine the access it needed to begin production.

silent. Despite some dewatering of the shaft in 1928 and diamond drilling for new deposits in 1942 and 1946, there was no further mining.

The post-war years would be the boom years for Burchell Lake. In 1951 a company called Coldstream Copper began to show some interest. It optioned the site and in 1956 constructed a 1,000-ton concentrator, but the financially shaky company still lacked funds to begin actual mining. Finally in 1959 L. R. Redford and G. H. MacDonald salvaged the operation, added a new electric pump and laid out an elaborate townsite which they called Burchell Lake.

By the lake, on Pollock's old village site, they constructed 11 log homes of special double-tongued British Columbia cedar. Their floors were polished hardwood; their ceilings open-beamed. In the shadow of the concentrator on curved suburban-like streets, they added 24 modest, but modern bungalows and 17 mobile homes. Beside the mine gate were four bunkhouses. A pump house and lagoon provided water and sewage facilities, while mercury vapour lights kept the site bright. Unlike their counterparts of a half-century earlier, mining men of the 1950s enjoyed shorter shifts and five-day work weeks. This increase in leisure time meant there was a need for recreational facilities. The men of Burchell Lake could curl, play baseball or challenge their rivals in nearby lumber towns to hockey on their own rink. Of course they could always shoot a leisurely game of pool in Kaski's general store. Of the mining towns in northwestern Ontario Burchell Lake was one of the largest and most modern, but its life would be short.

The Coldstream mine produced steadily. In just five years it yielded copper, gold and silver worth $28 million. But on August 5, 1966, a depressed market again forced the mine to close and the townsfolk to

147

A piece of 1950s nostalgia greets the visitor to Burchell Lake. Like the British-American Oil Company, this town exists only for ghosts.

These oil cans were left behind in the BA station when Burchell Lake was abandoned.

148

leave. G. H. MacDonald, the mine's manager wrote, "It is hoped that the remaining plant and equipment, including the townsite, can be disposed of at the best prices available."

MacDonald's hope has not yet been realized. Although the trailers are gone, the bunkhouses dismantled and the store demolished, much of the town remains intact. The bungalows still line the curving streets, their yards overgrown. Rusting fire hydrants hide in tall grass, while beside the school young trees push through the mesh of the baseball cage. The concentrator appears well-maintained and secure behind a padlocked gate.

At the end of Highway 802, at the entrance to the town, is a 1950s style "BA" gas station. Its windows broken and its white paint peeling, it appears to have been abandoned in a hurry for cans of oil still line its shelves. Nevertheless Burchell Lake has suffered little vandalism and is one of the best preserved of Ontario's recent ghost towns.

This curving street of modern-style bungalows still gives Burchell Lake a strangely suburban appearance.

BANKFIELD

North of Lake Superior and east of Lake Nipigon, Ontario's landscape is flat. No viewpoints or rocky cliffs beckon the holidayer or photographer. However, in the bleak fall and spring of 1931-32 prospectors Tom Johnson and Bob Wells were attracted by something else.

"About the end of September, 1931, I was out to Tashota," recalls Johnson, "and heard about the (gold) find at Little Longlac... I asked Bob Wells if he would like to take a trip with me... In cruising the shore I noticed an outcrop in the lake... the first piece I broke off was well mineralized... I told Wells I thought we had something of importance."

Johnson's "something of importance" proved to be the Bankfield gold field. In June, 1934 C. D. MacAlpine incorporated the Bankfield Gold Mining Company. He placed J. W. McKenzie in charge of operations and began work. At first Bankfield contained, in addition to the usual mine buildings, a dining hall and a few bunkhouses. But by 1937 it was developing into a sizeable town. In that year a $7,000 road was pushed 16-kilometers (10-miles) east to the big strike at Little Longlac where a railway village called Geraldton was becoming the hub of the new gold field.

In 1937 Bankfield added a 100-ton mill and townsite. Most of the 35 dwellings were neatly arranged around a crescent off the Geraldton road. Others were scattered haphazardly along the road. After a gruelling shift in the mine or mill, workers would gather at the recreation hall for badminton or tennis. During the long winter, the Bankfield Millionaires hockey team provided keen competition for neighbouring Geraldton,

This view of the Bankfield headframe and some of the village was taken during the mine's heyday in the 1930s.

Most of Bankfield's buildings have vanished. This survivor lingers precariously beside what were the mill buildings.

Two ghostly survivors of the Little Longlac gold rush have created an unusual skyline near Geraldton.

Jellicoe or Beardmore teams. For the town's native people, there was the Thunderbird Friendship Centre. The entire site was powered by electricity from the Cameron Falls power house five kilometers (3 miles) away.

For ten years Bankfield's production rivalled that at Little Longlac. During this time other mines with names like Jellicoe, Tombill and Magnet sprang up around Bankfield each with it own small townsite.

These were short-lived for wartime recruitment drained away much of their labour force. Even Bankfield was forced to close for two years and when it reopened, it was only for another three years. Despite Bankfield's intermittent operations, one of Ontario's deepest shafts, 400 meters (¼ mile), was sunk here and 66,000 ounces of gold and 7,500 ounces of silver hauled from it. In 1947 Bankfield closed for good. Families fled to Geraldton to work in the Little Longlac mines. Many trucked their houses piece by piece along the Geraldton road.

A new road, Highway 11, now bypasses the old Geraldton Road. Along the old route lies the rubble that was Bankfield. The tailings have been flattened, the townsite crescent is now a trail through a young poplar stand. At the mine sites, large concrete shells and foundations testify to the magnitude and the promise this gold field once held.

The clutch of mines south of Geraldton has also run dry. Here a forest of rusting headframes looms above the trees while at their feet the mine buildings sit gaunt and empty.

The Bankfield Millionaires hockey team provided competition for the growing communities in the Longlac gold field.

LEITCH

In 1934, prospector Russ Cyderman joined the rush to the Little Longlac gold fields. His explorations led him 80 kilometers (50 miles) west of the original strike to the shores of Lake Nipigon where, on two rocky outcrops, he found gold. His strike sparked the growth of one of Ontario's longest producing mines and a busy town. Today the site is little more than rubble.

In 1935 the Sand River mine sank its first shaft. A year later the Leitch mine began operations on the adjacent claim and soon its mill began grinding out 65 tons of gold ore each day. In 1937 the Leitch Gold Mining Company built seven bungalows overlooking the mine. A few years later it opened a second townsite one kilometer away where two dozen modern homes on curving streets gave the appearance of suburbia. Meanwhile, beside the mine, the company built a store, school, community hall and more houses. Because a 1909 Ontario law prohibited liquor in mining towns, recreation revolved around the baseball or hockey teams. For refreshment miners travelled to the railway town of Beardmore, five kilometers (3 miles) away.

In 1946, the Second World War over, the men drifted away and production slowed. "Operations reached an all-time low at midsummer,"

An early view of the long-lived Leitch headframe and mine buildings.

153

The mine office at the largely demolished townsite of Leitch.

lamented Leitch manager, G. A. McKay. "The return of temporary workers to the farms in Manitoba and a sudden drift of men immediately after VE Day left a bare minimum crew required to continue operation."

Two years later the men were back and production was on the upswing. A happier McKay reported, "The community at the mine has grown considerably, with an increase in families as well as single men. Housing sites and recreation ground are being improved as conditions permit."

In 1948 the Sand River mine closed, its reserves dry. Friends bade farewell and moved off to Beardmore to catch the train for new fields at Porcupine or Red Lake. The reserves at Leitch would last for 20 years longer and workers continued to arrive. By 1961 Canada's census-takers recorded 200 permanent residents. Production also grew and by 1965 Leitch had dug out 847,000 ounces of gold and 31,000 ounces of silver. With 30 years of operation, it was one of Ontario's longest producing mines.

Time finally ran out on the Leitch. In February, 1965 the miners emerged from the dark shafts for the last time and on June 15 the mill ground to a halt. A ringing silence pervaded the site. Slowly the Leitch residents bundled their furniture and memories into trunks, trailers and cars and, farewells said, drove off to various destinations.

Mine buildings were disassembled. Residents in nearby Jellicoe and Beardmore bought the Leitch homes and moved them onto private lots, but with the railway reducing its operations, Beardmore was in decline too, its false-fronted store shuttered and still.

At the mine, Leitch's remains cover several acres. Beside a deteriorating Highway 580, extensive foundations, rubble and a few shells mark the mine site. Along the quiet curving streets of the two townsites, a young forest has started to reclaim yards and basement foundations. It is said there is gold in the tailings. As gold prices rise the tailings may themselves become viable and Leitch may yet have another chapter in its story.

THERESA

Once the Little Longlac gold field was fully staked, prospectors ventured further afield. Forty kilometers (25 miles) east, amid a flurry of claim staking, grew the short-lived town of Theresa. From a tiny station village on the CNR called Longlac, prospectors made their way up the Making Ground River. Of the 37 mining claims staked on the Making Ground, the Theresa had the "most important showing" according to an Ontario Department of Mines report.

In 1937 N. A. Timmins optioned the claim and in 1938 mining began. With a modest force of 34 under the firm hand of foreman F. C. Tomlinson, a mill, bunkhouse, dining hall and four dwellings were built. It was called Theresa. Like the early prospectors, Tomlinson and his men had only the river as their highway.

During the war the Theresa mine saw only intermittent production. In 1947 when a new eight-kilometer (5-mile) road from Longlac removed the uncertainty and slowness of river travel, Theresa boomed into a busy mining town. Overlooking the river stood a new 100-ton mill and various mine buildings; 19 workers' dwellings lined a half-dozen village streets. The mining executives chose to remain aloof from the village and built their five homes on a knoll a kilometer away. Although the town also contained a community hall, many preferred the taverns of Longlac.

In 1949 A. Caouette succeeded Timmins and refitted the mill. Ther-

Mill machinery litters the site of the Theresa mine.

esa's production jumped to nearly 2,000 tons of ore in that year alone. Yet just four years later the Theresa was silent. The 5,600 tons of ore hauled out that year showed only meagre amounts of gold spelling economic doom for the operation. Bustling Longlac nearby provided new jobs and Theresa was quickly abandoned. Only two homes are still used.

The northern route of the Trans Canada Highway has largely replaced the railway and Longlac continues to boom. Most of the homes that stood in Theresa have now been moved closer to the new town. Theresa's streets remain clear and open, along them shells and foundations abound and mine machinery litters the landscape. Still standing in good repair are the executive homes, alone now on their exclusive little hill.

Most of Theresa's houses were moved or burned leaving roads lined with foundations.

PICKLE CROW
CENTRAL PATRICIA

Smoke billowed into the northern sky. Yellow flames crackled and danced in the vacant windows. One house, then another, collapsed in flames until wisps of smoke circled from the smouldering ruins of 33 homes. Pickle Crow lay in ashes. Neither a forest fire nor vandals burned the empty town, but Ontario's Ministry of Natural Resources. At the end of Ontario's most northerly highway, Pickle Crow was one of a trio of gold mining towns that included Pickle Lake, a community still very much alive and the sleepy half-abandoned Central Patricia. All were products of the great 1930s gold rush.

In 1928 the drone of aircraft grew louder over the tamaracks. Among the first passengers were prospectors John MacFarlane and H. H. Howell of Northern Aerial Minerals Exploration Ltd. They quickly struck gold on the banks of the Crow River and staked the area's first claims. Less than 12 months later on a single 18-kilometer (11-mile) stretch of the Crow River, more than 225 claims had been staked.

Despite this first flurry of activity, only three mining companies emerged: the Albany, the Central Patricia and the Pickle Crow. With no roads they were forced to follow a complicated water route for transportation. From Hudson on the CNR, 300 kilometers (180 miles) north-

A row of identical company homes lines Pickle Crow's main street beside the community centre before they were burned by the Ministry of Natural Resources in the early 1970s.

The village of Root Bay marked the terminus of a marine railway which before the highway was the only access to the Pickle Lake gold field.

west of Thunder Bay, the Lake St. Joseph Transportation Company barged every piece of equipment east over Lac Seul to a five-kilometer (3-mile) series of marine railways called the Root River Railway. At three different sites before they reached Lake St. Joseph, each barge was floated on top of a submerged rail car and hauled up an incline on standard-gauge rails before it was refloated. From Doghole Bay at the east end of Lake St. Joseph a truck road led the last 40 kilometers (24 miles) to the Pickle Crow mines. It was a tedious journey that on the average took 40 days and cost companies $35 for every ton moved. Even with these high start-up costs, the economic prospects of the gold fields looked excellent.

By 1934 the equipment was in place and the three towns began to take shape. By 1936 the "town" of Pickle Crow had little more than a bunkhouse and a handful of dwellings. In 1938 the Pickle Crow mining company took over the Albany production and tripled the capacity of its mill to 400 tons a day. Stretching along the single one-kilometer street more than 100 frame bungalows faced each other. The white, four-room homes rented for $15-$25 per month. Near the lofty headframe clustered the town's core buildings: the hospital, school, general store, a Catholic church and several bunkhouses. After a gruelling week in the mines, the workers would unwind at the bowling alley or in the curling rink.

Eight kilometers (5 miles) southwest was the sister village of Central Patricia. Despite a modest start in 1933 with a mill that produced only 50 tons per day, it increased its capacity eight-fold in less than eight years. By 1941 the population was nearly 400 and 90 homes were arranged on a neat grid of streets. The main street featured a hotel, gas station, school and bunkhouses. Meanwhile, an upstart village called Pickle Lake was struggling into existence with a population of just 95.

Low wages and the instability of the war years drove away many miners, but after 1945 the Canadian Metal Mining Association found willing workers in war refugees. The mining companies increased their wages to $2,000 per year, a substantial income then and the two towns enjoyed a period of prosperity and stability.

Starting in 1934 the Central Pat yielded 670,000 ounces of gold and silver worth $23 million until, in 1951, it ran dry and the mills closed. The company sold the buildings, houses and the 90 lots. Many of the new owners dragged their frame homes off to new destinations, while others remained in the skeleton of the town they had known, and still others just turned their backs and left. By 1956 the population had plummeted to 51.

Meanwhile the Pickle Crow was becoming one of the richest gold mines the province had ever known,. Between 1935 and 1966 it wrenched from the earth 1½ million ounces of gold and silver worth more than $32 million. Finally, in 1966, the Pickle Crow mine ran dry. On August 29 the last bucket of ore was hoisted and in September the mill fell silent. In 1971, the last year Pickle Crow appeared in the census, its population was one, its long row of houses empty. When the mining company showed no interest in either reworking the mine or removing the houses, the Ministry of Natural Resources moved in and burned them.

In 1956 Highway 599 provided the region with its first road access. While Pickle Crow and Central Pat withered, Pickle Lake began to grow. Not only did it have its own mine, but the road brought with it the need for government jobs such as highway maintenance and police, and it brought tourists and lumbermen. Miners uprooted from Pickle Crow

The rooms in the Pickle Crow hotel were attractively furnished.

and Central Pat moved to the bustling new community boosting its population to over 200.

North of Pickle Lake lie the ruins of the two gold towns. At Pickle Crow, the Catholic church and manager's residence survived the Ministry's fire. They are, unfortunately, succumbing to vandals who have hauled away all available metal and wood and have even dynamited the girders on the headframe. The ruins of Pickle Crow are a sad legacy of vandalism by thoughtless individuals and government officials. Central Pat has recovered slightly. Although its population has edged back to about 100, more than half its lots lie vacant.

But what of Central Patricia's future? The vagaries of mining may well restore the bustle of its peak days. Rumours of new finds pass from person to person, old mines now closed may rumble back to life. Even now many of the once-empty houses have new residents, the empty lots new mobile homes.

At the foot of Lake St. Joseph, now isolated from any transportation route, sits "Root Bay". Its 15 empty log buildings date from the days when it was the busy terminus of the Root River Railway.

Commercial air service has now been introduced to Pickle Lake and the highway upgraded. The drive from Thunder Bay, however, takes six hours, one way.

While Central Patricia still has about 100 residents many of its lots and buildings stand vacant.

UCHI LAKE

As the great gold rush of the 1930s swept northwestern Ontario, tamarack swamps and spruce ridges suddenly became boom towns and peaceful railway villages swarmed with eager prospectors. At Red Lake, a watery lowland 160 kilometers (96 miles) north of Dryden, headframes inched above the treeline and spawned several new communities. Some have survived mine closings to become tourist and dormitory towns, but so remote were the mining towns of Uchi Lake, Jackson Manion and Casummit that once the mines closed, there was no reason to remain and the residents fled. The largest of this trio of ghost camps was Uchi Lake.

Although the Uchi Lake deposit first came to light in 1927, eight years would pass before J. E. Hamell formed the Uchi Gold Mining Company. For four years he battled remoteness and poor access. He barged men and machinery across Confederation Lake to a ramshackle landing town called Lost Bay where a rugged bush road led to the mine. In 1938 the Ontario government opened a new road which bypassed the cumbersome water route and led directly to the mine. In 1939 the town had only a headframe, cookery, staffhouse and three bunkhouses, but in 1942 Hamell took over the adjacent Havalda, Jalda and Grassett claims and the work force swelled to 350. Uchi Lake had become a boom town.

Near the mine Hamell laid out streets and built modest homes for the

Uchi's headframe and mill were dismantled when the mine closed in 1943.

The presses were kept busy at the Uchi Lake gold mine. By the time it closed in 1943, after 12 years of full operation, $57 million in gold at today's prices had been removed.

families that had begun to arrive. Don McGillis from Red Lake added a two-storey hotel which contained a Bank of Commerce and a barber shop, the Johnsons operated a general store and Charles Keith a sawmill. More families arrived at Uchi Lake and built their own homes on a dirt road some distance from the mine. With the influx of families and children Hamell recognized the need for a school and ordered one built. For recreation he provided the miners with a community hall and curling rink.

As a company town Uchi Lake was dry. Lost Bay, however, was wide open and quickly developed into the recreational outlet for the mine. There, at a place called the Halfway House, liquor and ladies were easily available and Lost Bay caroused while Uchi Lake slept.

Despite its size and promise, Uchi Lake was short-lived. In 1943, after pulling 114,000 ounces of gold from the ground, the hoists fell silent. Although most residents left, some who preferred the isolation stayed until time took its toll and the road gradually became impassable. Then even the diehards abandoned Uchi Lake for good.

Since the mine's closing, much of the town has disappeared. Mine buildings were disassembled and removed. Some houses were rebuilt on Confederation Lake as cottages. Snow eventually pushed through the rotting roofs of the recreation hall and curling rink, and in 1975 wind levelled the hotel and several other structures. At the rowdy Lost Bay only six buildings survive.

Lonely provincial Highway 105 leads northward to Red Lake, Ear Falls and the other early mining towns. Today they depend on the more reliable industries of tourism and logging for their livelihood, but the headframes and the mining buildings remain as silent reminders of the 1930s gold frenzy.

An abandoned bunkhouse at Uchi Lake.

BERENS RIVER

Amid the remote, nearly inaccessible tamarack forests of far northwestern Ontario sit a bowling alley and a swimming pool. Nearby are the bunkhouses and homes that 40 years ago 600 people called home. Today they survive virtually unaltered to make what is Ontario's most complete ghost town. Yet it is one of its least known and least accessible.

In 1935 gold fever raged across Ontario's northland. New towns and villages appeared in remote regions few knew existed. Prospectors and mining magnates walked, paddled or flew to the glittering distant strikes. To tap one gold find near Ontario's subarctic border with Manitoba, H. Dewitt Smith formed the Newmont Mining Company. Throughout 1936 small planes chugged over the treetops carrying men, machines and furniture and by January, 1937, Smith had in place not just his mine buildings, but a pair of bunkhouses, a dining hall, office and executive quarters.

The cost of air transport was prohibitive even then and Smith began to slash a road through the tamaracks from Berens River Landing on Lake Winnipeg. Although a seemingly straightforward engineering project, Smith's road brought the governments of Manitoba and Ontario into bitter conflict. Ontario refused to help pay for a road located in Mani-

The Berens River hoist and mill in the late 1930s when this was the most northerly mining community.

Many of the Berens River miners lived in these large bunkhouses.

toba, Manitoba refused to subsidize a road to a mine in Ontario from which Ontario would reap the royalties.

While the governments quarrelled Smith expanded his townsite. In 1940 he added a five-bed hospital, more bunkhouses and a sawmill. By then he had taken from the ground 5,800 ounces of gold and 177,000 ounces of silver.

Berens quickly grew from a mere mining camp into a self-sufficient town. In 1941 Smith spent $23,900 on an apartment building, $3,200 for a police station and $5,600 for a school. Powered by the falls on a nearby river, Berens River could claim its own hydro plant. To encourage employees to build homes in the townsite, Smith provided each with an $800 interest-free loan.

By 1942 the town was in full swing. The payroll numbered 210, the population 600. Lack of road and rail links and lack of scheduled commercial air service made Berens River Ontario's most isolated white settlement. However the pay was good and with nothing to spend it on the miners saw their savings grow.

Remoteness also caused restlessness. To relieve tensions Smith built a recreation hall with a swimming pool and a bowling alley. Liquor was prohibited and despite some smuggling, drunkenness was seldom a problem. For a time the town's name was confused with Favourable Lake, a trading post and Indian settlement on a nearby lake of the same name. Some maps still show Berens River as Favourable Lake.

Arctic-like winters that were long and cold meant a compact townsite. While the bunkhouses and recreation facilities huddled close to the mine buildings, the houses lined curved "streets" on an adjacent hilltop.

Despite temperatures that often plunged to −50°C, (−60°F) the work-

165

Much of the Berens River machinery has remained in place such as this furnace.

ers would crowd the mill doors awaiting their shift. The summers, although short, were hot, with enough daylight to see by, even at midnight. The inhabitants enjoyed trolling for trout during these long evenings although the ever-present clouds of black flies made most other outdoor activities a trial of patience.

In 1945 when the war ended, prices for metal fell and the work force dwindled to 164. Production continued for three more years. On August 31, 1948 Smith dismantled the plant and said farewell to his employees. For most the stay had been brief.

Berens River's remoteness has helped to preserve it. As it was then, the only access today is by chartered plane. With nowhere to move the buildings, no vandals to burn or pillage and a climate that is dry and cold, Berens River remains much as it was left. Except for a few mine buildings which were dismantled, the town, with houses and hospital sits silently. Its recreation hall with the bowling alley and swimming pool are still usable. As it has for 30 years it sits as if waiting for an unseen hand to turn on the lights and start the machinery.

Flights can be chartered from the town of Red Lake to South Trout Lake where the old freight road can still be followed five kilometers (3 miles) through the bush. At its end, known by very few, sits Ontario's most complete ghost town.

The tiny Berens River jail provided a cooling-off place when the pressures of the community's isolation grew too much.

EPILOGUE

Ontario's newspapers once more cry out the words "Gold Rush". Prospectors crash through the underbrush near Marathon and stumble over rock outcrops peering carefully for the tell-tale glitter. It is not, however, a gold rush that will produce ghost towns. For today's prospectors and miners are products of a mobile society. Literally. Camps, even townsites, now consist of uniform mobile homes that appear overnight and disappear just as quickly.

Ontario's ghost towns are a thing of the past. Even when today's industry abandons a community, the residents stay put, for their wide roads and fast cars will speed them to jobs in the next town.

In other parts of the country, there are ghost towns in the making. Ocean Falls, British Columbia, Uranium City, Alberta, and Schefferville, Quebec have seen their mines or mills close and their residents flee. Their homes are still firm, their appearance modern and the right economic injection may yet restore them to life.

But across Ontario and throughout the country, the old towns of wooden churches and false-fronted stores are rapidly deteriorating at the hands of weather and vandals and will eventually vanish. In American states and in other Canadian provinces governments have preserved the best. But as railways demolish their stations, as banks tear down their historic branches, as the Ministry of Natural Resources burns and bulldozes buildings on Crown Lands, Ontario's heritage is fast vanishing. Its ghost towns will be just one of the victims.

GLOSSARY

BARITE: A soft opaque crystal used as a filler in paint and in oil drilling.

BOARD FOOT: A unit equal to the cubic contents of a piece of wood one-foot square and one-inch thick.

DIVISIONAL TOWN: A railway facility that contains repair shops, maintenance yards and boarding facilities for train crews responsible for that portion of railway line, usually located 180 to 200 kilometers (115-125 miles) apart.

GOLD PRICES: Before 1931, gold prices were pegged at $20.67 and after 1934 at $35 per ounce. In the early 1970s, gold prices were allowed to float, peaking at over $800 per ounce in 1980. 1983 prices fluctuate between $400 and $450.

HEAD OF NAVIGATION: The farthest point on a river or body of water that a vessel can navigate.

HEADFRAME: A structure located directly above a mine shaft that contains hoists for workers and ore.

HIGH GRADING: A mining practice whereby only the highest concentrations of minerals are extracted, leaving the lower concentrations in place.

MACKINAW: A flat-bottomed, double-ended boat indigenous to the northern Great Lakes.

SECTION VILLAGE: A railway village consisting of maintenance sheds and quarters for a maintenance crew and foreman responsible for the repair of a 20-kilometer (12-mile) section of track.

SKIFF: A sailing or rowing boat small enough to be handled by one person.

SMACK: A small fishing boat that contains a well to keep the catch alive.

STAMP MILL: A mining building used to process ore by crushing and separating the mineral from the crushed rock.

WAY FREIGHT: A train consisting of freight and often passenger cars that delivers general goods and mail to towns and villages on the railway line.

PHOTO CREDITS

Algonquin Park Museum: pages 38, 39, 41, 42, 43, 95

Brown, Ron: pages 14, 17, 19, 21, 22, 25, 30, 32, 34, 45, 46, 51, 53, 54, 58, 59, 70, 74, 75, 78, 80, 82, 83, 86, 89, 90, 91, 92, 94, 96, 103, 106 (bottom), 109, 111, 112 (bottom), 113, 115, 116, 117, 122, 123, 129, 134, 142, 143 (bottom), 145, 148, 149, 151, 154, 155, 156

Canadian Lumberman & Woodworker: page 112 (top)

Department of Fisheries & Game: page 57

Dinsmore, K.: page 68

Goodmurphy, A.: page 52

Hastings County Museum: pages 27, 28

Lakehead University Archives: page 102

Lost Channel Lodge: pages 87, 88

MacDonald, L.: pages 84, 85

Metro Toronto Public Library: page 72

Ministry of Culture & Citizenship: pages 64, 158, 160, 163, 165, 166, 167

Ministry of Natural Resources: pages 33, 40, 44, 60, 105, 106 (top), 107, 108

Ontario Archives: pages 15, 48, 50, 61, 62, 63, 71, 76, 79 (top), 125, 126, 130, 131, 133, 136, 137

Ontario Bureau of Mines: pages 79 (bottom), 81, 119, 120, 121, 132, 138, 139, 141, 143 (top), 144, 146, 147, 150, 153

Ontario Department of Mines: pages 157, 159, 161, 162

Public Archives of Canada: pages 65, 101

Women's Institute: pages 18, 20

BIBLIOGRAPHY

Addison, Ottelyn, *Early Days in Algonquin Park*, Toronto.
Baldring, *Innovation Versus Invitation, Cobalt Through the Years*, n.d.
Bice, Ralph, *On the Trail in Algonquin Park*, Toronto, 1979.
Beckerton, L., et al, *History of Spanish*, Opportunities For Youth Project, Spanish, 1974.
Blackburn, K., et al. *Maritime History of the North Shore of Lake Huron*, Spanish, 1971.
Bradstreet Company, *The Mercantile Agency Reference Book*, Toronto, 1910.
Brown, Ron, *Ghost Towns of Ontario, Volume One*, Langley BC, 1978.
Brown, Ron, "Depot Harbour", *Canadian Geographic Journal*, December, 1977.
Buchan, Dilys, "Copper, Silver Gold and Solitude", *Fort Frances Times*, 1979.
Buchan, Dilys, "Shoal Lake's Golden Cities", *Fort Frances Times*, 1979.
Bullock, W.S., *Cobalt and its Silver Mines*, np, 1906.
Campbells Corners Women's Institute, *History of Bentinck Township*, nd np.
Campbell, Paul, and D.J. Cunning, "Mines and Mills at Gold Rock", *Continuity With Change*, Mark Fram and John Weiler ed, Toronto, 1981.
Campbell, William J., *Northeastern Georgian Bay and its People*, Sudbury, 1982.
Canadian Lumberman and Woodworker, various issues, Peterborough, various dates.
Cassidy, G.L., *Arrow North, The Story of Temiskaming*, Cobalt, 1976.
Coons, C.F., "The John R. Booth Story", *Your Forests*, Volume 2, Number 2, 1978.
"Cobalt", *The Toronto Globe*, Special Edition, Toronto, October 3, 1906.
Consolidated Mines Company of Lake Superior Ltd., Annual Report of the Porcupine Mine, Badger Mine, Keystone Mine, West End Silver Mountain, East End Silver Mountain, 1901.
Dominion Bureau of Statistics, Census of Canada, Population by Districts and Subdistricts, 1891, 1901, 1911, 1921, 1931, 1941, 1951, 1961.
Dominion Bureau of Statistics, List of Unincorporated Places, 1956 and 1951.
Dominion Bureau of Statistics, Population of Unincorporated Villages and Hamlets.
Dominion Bureau of Statistics, Unincorporated Places of Less Than 50 Persons, 1961 and 1966.
Dun and Bradstreet Company, *Mercantile Agency Reference Book*, Toronto, 1920, 1930.
Dun and Bradstreet of Canada, Reference Book, Toronto, 1950, 1960.
Eckersley, W., "The Steamboat Era on the Pickerel River", *Parry Sound North Star*, November 30, 1978.
Gard, Anson, *Gateway to Silverland*, Toronto, 1906.
Gard, Anson, *The Real Cobalt*, Toronto, 1908.
Georgian Bay Pilot, 1903.
Gibson, Thomas W., *Mining in Ontario*, Toronto 1937.
Hamilton, James C., *The Georgian Bay*, Toronto, 1893.
Kase, Ed, *Progress Through the Years*, np, nd.
Kauffman, Carl, *Logging Days in Blind River*, Sault Ste. Marie, 1970.
Kirton, E., "Lost Channel Just a Memory", *Parry Sound North Star*, June 26, 1975.
Lewis, Viola W., *History of Ardbeg*, ms, 1977.
Livingstone, J.C., *The Story of Silver Islet*, Fort William, nd.
MacDonald, J.E., *Yonder Our Island*, Thessalon, 1979.
MacFarlane, Leslie, "The Sun Also Sets", *Canadian Mining Journal*, 1933.
MacKay, Nial, *Over the Hills to Georgian Bay*, Boston Mills, 1982.

McKean, James, Depot Harbour, *Profile of a Railway Town*, unpublished essay, Waterloo, 1968.

Marsh, E.L., *A History of the County of Grey*, Owen Sound, 1967.

Mights Directory of Grey and Bruce, 1895.

Mights Directory of Northern Ontario, 1928.

Mika, Nick and Helma, ed., *Community Spotlight*, Belleville, 1974.

Ontario Bureau of Mines, Annual Reports, 1892-1920, Toronto.

Ontario Department of Lands and Forests, District Histories, Various dates, Toronto.

Ontario Department of Mines, Annual Reports, 1921-1968, Toronto.

Ontario Department of Mines, "North Coldstream Mines, Ltd., Burchell Lake", Toronto 1967.

Pain, S.A., *The Way North*, Toronto, 1964.

Parrott, D.L., *The Red Lake Gold Rush*, 1976.

Platel, Rudy, "Death of Algonquin Hamlet Postponed", *Toronto Globe and Mail*, February 6, 1979.

Poole, Jane, *Jackfish*, np, Terrace Bay, 1976.

Pye, E.G., Geology and Scenery, Rainy Lake East to Lake Superior, Geological Guide Book Number 1, Ontario Department of Mines, 1968.

Reynolds, Nila, *In Quest of Yesterday*, Haliburton.

Robertson, Norman, *History of the County of Bruce*, Walkerton, 1906.

Sault Star, "Early Days Reveal Spragge as a Lumber Town", Sault Ste. Marie, 1959.

Scott, James, *The Settlement of Huron County*, Toronto, 1966.

Smith, D.H., "The Stolen Sawmill", Sylva, Ontario Department of Lands and Forests Review, nd.

Statistics Canada, Ontario Listing of Places with Zero Population, 1971.

Statistics Canada, Ontario Listing of Unincorporated Places 49 Persons and less, 1971.

Strickland, Helen M., *Silver Under the Sea*, Cobalt, 1979.

Thorpe, T., A Review of Logging and Pulp Operations in Sudbury District, During the Years 1901-1950, Ontario Department of Lands and Forests, nd.

Tough, George W., Rise and Decline, Hamlets and their Hinterlands in a Small Shield Area, Unpublished BA Thesis, University of Western Ontario, London, 1964.

Tucker, Albert, *Steam Into Wilderness*, Toronto, 1978.

Wooden, Joseph L., *A Drum to Beat Upon*, Exeter, 1971.

INDEX

Aberdeen............... 18-19
Algoma Central Railway .. 8, 99
Algonquin Park...... 38-44, 91,
    94-97
Ardbeg 84-86
Austin, James.........105-110,
    111, 113

Bankfield..........100, 150-152
Barnet, A.....................43
Beatty, Wm 49
Bell, Dr. MacIntosh ... 121-122
Bell City............... 135-137
Berczy, William............... 9
Berens River......100, 164-167
Bigmaster Mine........ 141-145
Bobcaygeon Road 33
Booth, John Rudolphus 38,
    45, 47-50
Booth Line Railway 38, 43,
    44, 46, 49
Brent 91-93
Brule Lake............... 43-44
Buckhorn Road..............33
Burchell Lake.......... 146-149
Burleigh Road 31, 32
Burnt Island 59
Bustard Islands.......56, 60-61

Canada Atlantic
    Railway 47, 49
Canadian Northern
    Railway 8, 38, 99
Cantin, Narcisse 12-15
Cassumit Mine.........100, 161
Central Patricia ...100, 157-160
Cheddar................... 31-32
Chief City 137

Cockburn Island.......... 51-55
Coldstream Copper Mine.. 147
Collier, Earl..................27
Cooper, James................27
Crawford, James...... 18-19, 24

Dalton Mills............ 111-113
Dalton Station 111-113
Daunais, Oliver............. 130
Depot Harbour.......38, 47-50
Detola Mine........... 144-145
Duff, P.S.................. 43-44

Fassett Lumber Company ...94
Fitzwilliam Island......... 56-57
Foley.................. 137-139
Fosmill.................... 94-95
Foster, William 94
Fraser, Shannon..............41
French River.............. 71-73
Frue, William 127-128

Gelert..................... 33-34
Gillies Hill................. 22-23
Gillies, John............... 22-23
Glammis................... 24-25
Gold Rock.......... 8, 141-145
Great Duck Island....... 56, 58

Hamilton, James Cleland ... 56,
    57, 60, 71
Havilah Gold Mining Co 82
Horwood Lake........ 114-115

Jackfish................. 101-104
Jackson-Manion 100, 161
John Island 66-67
Johnson, Tom 150

Kalamazoo Vegetable &
 Parchment Co 117-118
Kennedy, Black Jack 87
Key Valley Railway 88-90
Kiosk 94-97

Lake St. Joseph Transportation
 Co....................... 158
Lanark Societies 9
Laurentian Mine....... 142-145
Leitch.............100, 153-154
Little Longlac......... 100, 150,
                      152, 156
Lost Bay.................... 162
Lost Channel............. 87-90
Lyons, R.A. 68-69

Malcolm 20-21, 22
Michaels Bay.............. 68-70
Mine Centre 133-139
Monck Road 32
Mond, Ludwig............... 78
Mowat 38-44
Mowat Lodge 41-42
Moyles Mills.............. 66-67

National Transcontinental
 Railway 99
Nicholson 7, 8, 105-110
Nicholson, George.....105-110,
                      111, 113
Nipissing Road 46

Olive Mine 138
Ontario Lumber Co. 71, 73
Ontario Northland
 Railway....................99
Ontario Radium
 Corporation...............31
Ophir.................... 81-83
Ottawa, Arnprior and Parry
 Sound Railway............38

Pakesley 87-89
Parry Hoot...................49
Parry Sound 47-50
Petworth................... 29-30
Pickle Crow 100, 157-160

Pickle Lake........100, 157-160
Pinelands Lumber
 Co..................... 114-115
Port Milford 27-28
Purvis Brothers........... 58-59

Rathbun Lumber Co. 29
Robinson, Peter............... 9
Rock Lake................ 42-43
Root River Railway....158, 160

St. Joseph 12-15
St. Joseph and Sratford Radial
 Railway 13
Sable and Spanish River Boom
 & Lumber Co. 64
Seguin Falls 45-46
Seine City 135, 137
Sibley, Major
 Alexander........... 127-129
Silver Centre.......... 119-123
Silver Islet.........100, 124-129
Silver Mountain 130-132
Spragge.................... 74-77
Spanish Mills..........62-65, 66
Squaw Island.............. 56-57
Staniforth, S.J............. 94-96

Talbot, James.................. 9
Temiskaming & Northern
 Ontario Railway .. 8, 99, 122
Theresa................. 155-156
Thirty Thousand Islands 35
Thomson, Tom........... 41-42
Tionaga 114-115
Tip Top Mine 146
Tolsma, Zebe 51-55
Tolsmaville................ 52-55
Tophet 116-120
Toronto Grey & Bruce
 Railway....................16
Toronto Northern
 Railway 35, 56
Tudhope & Ludgate Co. 84
Turtle City 137

Uchi Lake........100, 161-163

Vankoughnet, Peter..........45
Victoria Harbour
    Lumber Co.................87
Victoria Mines............ 78-80
Victoria Railway 33

Wabb, Sam....................71
Wabigoon 143
Wood, Benjamin..............31
Wroxeter................. 16-17

W<small>E</small> hope you have enjoyed *Ghost Towns of Ontario, Volume 2.* Other books by Ron Brown include:

Ghost Towns of Ontario, Volume One	
(Southern and Eastern Ontario)	*$11.95 paperback*
Ghost Towns of Ontario: A Field Guide	*$12.95 paperback*
Ghost Towns of Canada	*$19.95 paperback*

• • •

Other books about Ontario are also published by *CannonBooks:*

More Bill Bramah's Ontario	*$10.95 paperback*
Bill Bramah's Ontario	*$10.95 paperback*
Bill Bramah's Nooks & Crannies	*$10.95 paperback*

Bill Bramah is best-known as Global TV's roving reporter. He has travelled hundreds of thousands of miles throughout Ontario finding interesting people and places.

A journalist for over 50 years, his warm and witty stories have delighted generations.

Memories of Ontario by Terry Boyle *$14.95 paperback*

The tourist on holiday, the armchair traveller and anyone interested in our heritage will find Terry Boyle's "mini-histories" of 73 western Ontario cities and towns valuable glimpses of a past rich with character and drama.

• • •

If you are unable to find these books in a bookstore near you, you may order them from the address below. Please enclose payment, payable to B<small>OOKS</small> B<small>Y</small> M<small>AIL</small>, the titles of the books you want, and your name and full mailing address.

B<small>OOKS</small> B<small>Y</small> M<small>AIL</small>
P.O. Box 1700, Station R
Toronto, Ontario M4G 4A3